"Through practical words, key illustrations, and a mixture of Scripture and guidance, Mary Busha's book will assist readers in finding freedom in their lives."

Dr. Michael Sedler, author and speaker

"As a board-certified clinical neuropsychologist, I daily have the opportunity to see how words have the power to either build up or tear down—and either can have a lasting impact for decades. In *The Healing Power of Positive Words*, Mary Busha gently guides the reader through the process of understanding the motive behind words, following the path to forgiveness, embracing their true identity, and walking into the freedom provided by God's Word. She points out to readers the impact not only of words spoken to them but also of their words spoken to themselves and others. This is the book for those truly desiring to heal from the power of negative words."

Dr. Michelle Bengtson, board-certified clinical neuropsychologist and author of the award-winning *Hope Prevails*, the *Hope Prevails Bible Study*, and *Breaking Anxiety's Grip*

the
healing
power of
positive
words

the
healing
power of
positive
words

mary c. **busha**

SPIRE

© 2019 by Mary Busha

Published by Revell
a division of Baker Publishing Group
PO Box 6287, Grand Rapids, MI 49516-6287
www.revellbooks.com

Spire edition published 2022
ISBN 978-0-8007-4117-4
eISBN 978-1-4934-3590-6

Previously published in 2019 under the title *Breaking the Power of Negative Words*

Printed in the United States of America

22   23   24   25   26   27   28   7   6   5   4   3   2   1

To the loving memory of
Lazar and Catherine Abraham,
whose DNA our all-knowing heavenly Father blended
when he knit my parts together and created me
for such a time as this.

contents

PART 3 words we speak to others

preface

words—they're everywhere!

From the moment we arise to when we go to sleep at night, and at all hours in between, words come at us from every direction. If not someone else's words, then the words are our own, words we think or say to ourselves. All too often, the words are not positive.

Why? We live in a fallen world. We're not perfect human beings. We get weary. We get hurt. We get angry. And it's often out of these conditions that words leap from our mouths to land, often unsuspectingly, on other human beings. I've been there. I've had extremely hurtful words flung at me. And I've hurled a few myself. They're words such as:

You'll never amount to anything.
Why can't you be more like your brother?
Why do you break everything you touch?

11

That was good, but you could have done better.

You'll never make it without me.

I don't love you.

You're too fat.

And the list goes on. Some words spoken to some of you are far more hurtful and abusive by comparison.

Where do these words come from? Scripture tells us that out of the abundance of the heart the mouth speaks (Luke 6:45). If that's the case, then from my observations, we have a lot of people with damaged hearts—not in the physical sense, of course, but spiritually and emotionally.

In my research for this book and from the interviews I've held, this is exactly what I've found. There are a great number of people walking around with some level of heartbrokenness. Hurt at one time or another by someone else, they (we) in turn hurt others, often with words. It's a vicious cycle that leaves a vast amount of collateral damage in homes, businesses, schools, and other arenas every day. And the effects carry long into our futures.

Words are powerful. In fact, the Bible tells us that our tongues have the power of life or death (Prov. 18:21). I can testify that when comforting words, encouraging words, words of life are spoken to me, I feel as though I can do and be anything and everything. When hurtful words, insulting words—in essence, words of death—are spoken to me, I cringe both inside and out, and something inside me tends to wither and die, such as aspirations, dreams, longings, and, worse, my self-worth.

Certainly, as you reach back into your memory bank, you too can recall times when words of life were spoken to you.

Do you recall how good they made you feel? On the other hand, unless you've lived in a bubble, you must admit to times when you were stung by someone's words. How did you feel then? Hurt, angry, defeated, rebellious? It would be natural to experience one or all of those feelings and many other emotions as well.

But now what? What do we do once we attest to having been the recipients or dispensers of harmful, hurtful, and, in some cases, death-giving words? One thing we could do is form a woe-is-me club and walk around as victims the rest of our lives. Or we could act as though the harmful words of others don't bother us, as we file them away into a corner of our already broken hearts. Or, and this is what I suggest, we could take steps to try to understand why the words were spoken in the first place and then take additional strides toward healing and freedom.

I've known about the impact of words for a long time, having worked in the publishing industry for most of my professional life. But only recently have I looked personally at just how much power they contain. What stands out most are words spoken to us early in our lives, which I call in chapter 1 *childhood mottos*.

It would not surprise me if most of you reading thus far could look back and add words you remember, words that felt like daggers to your heart and words that may even cause you to question your existence. I certainly can. Those expressions generally lurk just beneath the surface, merely waiting for a prompt to remind us of their sting. And with each reminder, the words become even more embedded in the fiber of who we are and subsequently motivate us to do what we do—or not do.

My intention is not merely to bring to remembrance words from our pasts. Rather, my aim is to take us beyond the words and offer steps that can help remove their harmful effects and place us on a pathway to healing and freedom.

I'm beginning to believe we all need this message, if not to heal then to celebrate the words of encouragement from others and thank the ones who issued those words. If nothing else, there's a strong reminder to be mindful of the words we speak. I don't know about you, but I don't want to issue deadly words. I want my words to offer life. I want my words to help heal broken people and to encourage them to experience all God has for them.

The effects of someone's spoken words can go deep and cause considerable and long-term damage, so what I offer throughout this book is not meant to oversimplify the healing of something as dramatic as a broken heart caused by hurting words. In addition, this book is not meant to take the place of counseling, therapy, or any other form of treatment or recovery process. I do believe, however, the concepts I share can help unlock doors that lead to a better understanding of why the hurtful words were spoken in the first place and then ultimately to a measure of healing.

As we explore the reasons behind hurting words in part 1 and what to do to nullify their effects, we'll see that we can grow from our experiences and make positive choices about what we allow into our lives. In part 2, we look at the words we speak to ourselves—self-talk. You may be surprised, or not, at the negativity we feed ourselves. Then in part 3, we delve into the topic of what we speak to others and how our words negatively or positively influence the lives of those around us.

I invite you to join me on this journey of spoken words, and as you do, may you gain new understanding and fresh skills to deal with them. And if needed, may you begin your personal journey to break free from the power of negative and hurting words.

acknowledgments

First and foremost, thank you to my husband, Bob, who supported me from day one with his love, words of encouragement, and complete consideration.

To my children, other family members, and friends, who gave me their reassurance of love and encouragement, thank you.

To my writer friends and readers close by and around the country, thank you for your support, fresh eyes, and great suggestions.

To those who shared their stories so that together we can encourage the hearts of others, my deepest thanks.

To Lonnie Hull-DuPont and the entire Baker team, my sincere gratitude for your belief in this work. I know it's your prayer as well as mine that many are blessed by the words contained within. Thank you too for your fine and professional work in bringing this book to market.

words spoken to us

Our words carry enormous weight. . . .
They often impact people for decades,
providing the courage to press on or one
more reason to give up.

MICHAEL HYATT

1

up close and personal

What we say to others today could influence them for years
to come, maybe for the rest of their lives.

It was a beautiful summer afternoon in Davison, a sleepy
little mid-Michigan town, where my husband and I had
moved to live near my aging mother. My friend Sally and
her mother-in-law, Olivia, drove from a neighboring city to
meet Mom and me for lunch. What a sweet time of sharing
and honoring the moms.

Near the end of lunch, almost in passing, my friend told us
about a young woman who had sung in her church the previous Sunday morning. Sally sighed and said she had always
wanted to sing like that. Then she asked her mother-in-law if
there was anything she had always desired. Without missing
a beat, Olivia said, "I've wanted to be pretty."

Her answer left the three of us a little disconcerted, primarily because she didn't have to think about her response. It just came out. We tried to assure her that she was pretty both inside and out. But our words seemed to fade into oblivion as she went on to explain that when she was quite young, her mother became gravely ill, leaving her teen sister to take over the household. Olivia shared that when she went to her older sister with a request, often her sister said to her, "You're homely."

Practically in unison, the three of us said, "Really?"

What cruel words to say to a little girl. No female of any age wants to be told she's homely. If anything, inherently, we all want to believe we are beautiful. The tragedy, however, is that nearly eighty years later, those words, "You're homely," were still so close to the surface.

While we may never know specifically how those words influenced Olivia over the years, we know they must have had at least some effect on her esteem and self-worth. Adult women would be shattered to hear those words. However, we might at least know better how to deal with them. But a little girl takes in what she hears and, because she is too young to process all the ins and outs of what was said, she most often will allow the words into her psyche and begin to believe them. Olivia certainly must have felt "less than" many times in her life. It appears the older sister sentenced her little sister to a prison of words, words just waiting to escape.

Another woman shared her own set of words when my husband, Bob, taught a writing class at an assisted-living residence. Teaching on the difference between impressive and expressive writing, he instructed that while impressive writing is for the eyes of others, expressive writing is for the writer only. He explained that expressive writing done on a regular basis has been shown to bring healing to the writer. He asked if anyone wanted to write about something in their past that may have caused them hurt or deep emotional stress.

Just like Olivia, Marilyn spoke up immediately. "I do," she said. She then proceeded to tell Bob and the others about a young girl on the playground when Marilyn was in elementary school. The other girl, who was swinging, shouted that she was done with the swing and anyone could have it. "Anyone but Marilyn," she added.

And Marilyn carried those words and their effects with her throughout elementary school, junior high school, high school, and well into adulthood. Words spoken to Marilyn when she was around ten still haunted her into her eighties.

Olivia and Marilyn didn't realize that the words spoken to them when they were still so young may have caused something deep inside to wither and die: their self-esteem, their self-worth, their need for significance. And they both carried those words into the winter of their lives.

I use Olivia's and Marilyn's stories to show how long hurtful words can stay with us. But following are examples of younger individuals.

Rich Mullins, the oldest son of an Indiana farmer, became well known in the 1970s and '80s for his musical gift of singing and songwriting. Not only did he record and make his songs popular, but so did many other Christian artists and groups over the years, songs such as "Awesome God" and "Sing Your Praise to the Lord." Early on, Rich's father expected his son to carry on the farming tradition and tried hard to groom him, but to no avail. The young Mullins had other aspirations, and they didn't line up with his father's plans.

When Rich tried to please his father, attempting to perform simple chores around the farm, he was clumsy, sometimes breaking his dad's coveted machinery. This led to extreme disappointment in the eyes of the father who issued harsh words to his son, such as "Everything you touch gets broken!" In a description of the movie *Ragamuffin*, about the life of Rich Mullins, it's written: "Rich wrestled all of his life with the brokenness and crippling insecurity born of his childhood."[1] He went on to suffer brokenness in many areas of his life before his early death at the age of forty-one.

Likewise, once-professing atheist Lee Strobel, author of the book *The Case for Christ*, experienced a rocky relationship with his father. Lee explains in an interview prior to the 2017 release of the movie by the same name that the night before he was to graduate from high school, he argued with his father. Before Lee stormed out of the house, his father told him he didn't have enough love for Lee to fill his little finger.

Although Lee did not attribute his becoming a staunch atheist solely to this broken relationship with his father, he shared in an interview that he believes there was an emotional as well as an intellectual underpinning in his decision not to believe in and seek after a heavenly Father.[2] Unfortunately, the rift between Lee and his father never fully healed before his father's death.

Yes, words go deep and can cause considerable damage.

Childhood Mottos

Early in the writing of this manuscript, I stumbled across a book in a local thrift shop. The title, *Putting Away Childish*

Things,[3] piqued my interest. Scanning its pages, I read excerpts about childhood mottos we hear early in life that rule us indefinitely unless we recognize the words for what they are and rid them from our lives. Dr. David A. Seamands wrote his book in 1982, but its message is as relevant today as it was then.

Childhood mottos that are normally spoken to us say or imply such ideas as:

> *That was good, but you could have done better.*
> *You're just not as smart as your sister.*
> *You'll never amount to anything.*
> *Everything you touch gets broken.*
> *Can't you do anything right?*

We listed some of these mottos in the preface. Can you add a childhood motto or two of your own? I certainly can. And I'll share some of mine later in this chapter.

Brad's Story

For now, I want to share about Brad, a pastor whom Dr. Seamands met prior to writing his book. Brad said that for many years he had been a "struggling, up-and-down Christian." Outwardly, he was a successful pastor with a record of considerable accomplishments. Inwardly, however, he was like a yo-yo, bouncing between spiritual highs and lows. "Or," he said, "like a billiard ball batting from one side to another, hitting pride on one side and condemnation, guilt, and depression on the other."

One day Brad realized his life was not really being ruled by love for God and others. Rather, for forty-nine years, a childhood motto instilled in him by his parents ran his life. What was the motto Brad adopted in his early years? "Measure up!"

Brad continued, "I'm sure my parents didn't mean to give me this impression, but what I heard them saying was, 'Sure, we love you, but we would love you more if only you would measure up!'"[4]

Aware now of what had been the guiding force for so many years, Brad saw how those two simple words affected him in all his relationships, including his relationship with the Lord. For so long, no matter his accomplishments, he did not believe he could measure up. Once those words were exposed, he was able to start a process of reconciliation and recovery.

I wonder how many other Christians are walking around who are just like Brad—confessing the Good News of Jesus but bound up in a prison of words. Perhaps too many of us to count. We know the truth of the gospel, but we do not walk in the freedom it provides.

My Childhood Mottos

Here is a childhood motto I grew up with: "If you can't eat it, don't buy it." Yes, you read it right. My mom, in her practicality, was saying to spend money on food and not on nonessentials. Of course, then I didn't understand what was behind Mom's words. I just took them in and did the best I could to comply. For many years, I found it much easier to buy groceries or go out for a meal than to shop for a dress or a new pair of shoes. Often, I felt practically paralyzed entering a department store. Believe me, there is power in spoken words.

Here's another motto. Whenever we called on family or friends, Mom prefaced our visit with the words "Don't ask for anything, and if something is offered, say, 'no, thank you.'" Imagine a little girl wanting a drink of water, for example, but too afraid and ashamed to ask. Or consider her being offered one of her favorite almond windmill cookies but having to refuse it. That was little Mary growing up.

In my Assyrian culture, as in many cultures, when you visit, the first thing the hostess does is put on the teakettle and bring out cakes or cookies. Oh, the angst I felt when we visited anywhere, anticipating the litany that always preceded and followed our arrival. Of course, the older person always won, and finally, I was permitted to accept what was offered.

Some of my earliest memories are the weekly visits to Grandpa and Grandma Essa. Each time, before we left to return home, Grandpa offered me a fifty-cent piece or a dollar bill. Each time, I said, "No, thank you." But Grandpa persisted and always got his way. How much easier it would have been for me to simply take his gift in the first place and say thank you. But no, the exact scene played out each time. I chuckle now, thinking about Grandpa, who, in his broken English and with furrowed brow, was determined not to be outmaneuvered by a child. But at the time, it was no laughing matter to this little girl.

Mom's words, "Don't ask for anything, and if something is offered, say, 'no, thank you'" are directly opposite of what the Scriptures tell us. Our generous heavenly Father wants to bestow gifts on His children. He says to ask, and it shall be given (Matt. 7:7). But how could I ask? I was told never to ask for anything. I was well into my adulthood before I could comfortably present my petitions to the Lord for my wants—even for some of my needs. Yes, words go deep.

Another childhood motto was "You're just like your father." Now, you need to know this was not meant as a compliment. Mom and Dad had a fitful seventeen-year marriage. Dad was a gambler. Most Fridays he did not come home with his paycheck. After a late night of poker, someone else's father took home the money we needed to pay our rent and purchase groceries for the following week.

Nonetheless, I loved my dad, and somehow we never went hungry or without a roof over our heads—thanks to the Lord and my mother's ingenuity. So hearing the words "You're just like your father" didn't affect me as much as the tone in which they were spoken. I was an obedient and compliant child, even in my teens, and when Mom spoke those words in that manner, it was hard for me to make sense of them. They were derisive words, implying that I, like Brad in our earlier example, didn't measure up to a standard, one I felt I never could attain.

I'm grateful that at nearly fifty years of age I recognized and began a process of no longer feeling the need to measure up—for there was nothing I could do to fulfill someone else's expectations—in order to gain the approval I obviously sought. It finally dawned on me that I was pleasing to my heavenly Father and that it was His love—and acceptance—that mattered.

Please note that I loved my mom and she loved me. There were reasons she did and said what she did. Her heart was broken as a child and wounded further as a young wife and mother. Sadly, Mom never fully healed from her soul injuries that resulted in her issuing hurtful words. Bottom line: hurt people hurt other people. This concept is not revolutionary or unique to this book. Others, more educated and qualified than I, have researched and found the presence of previous abuse in the lives of those who inflict abuse. It tends to perpetuate itself. In some ways, Mom could not help herself. Out of her hurt, she inflicted hurt.

We discuss this more in the next chapter as we look at the importance of reaching a level of understanding what is behind someone's stinging words. I cannot stress enough the importance of seeing the words for what they are instead of what we perceive them to be. Once we do, healing and freedom can begin.

Mom and I had a sweet relationship following my "cutting of the apron strings." She went to be with the Lord in June of 2016, and for the last several years of her life, my husband, Bob, and I, along with my sister, Paula, saw to her care, for which Mom was grateful—and for which we were equally thankful to be able to do.

Not All Childhood Mottos Are Negative

This discussion would not be complete if we looked only at childhood mottos that leave negative effects. Some are quite positive.

Take that of Mary Kay Ash, the successful businesswoman who pioneered and ran Mary Kay Cosmetics for many years. Mary Kay's childhood motto was "You can do it!" Her mother instilled those words in her daughter early on when it was necessary for Mary Kay to take over the care of her ill father once her mother took on full-time work. As young as five and six years old, she looked after the needs of her father.

Mary Kay's biography, *Miracles Happen*,[5] says that her mother phoned home from work to give instructions to her little girl on what to fix for dinner. Her mother always ended her call by saying, "You can do it!" And Mary Kay did.

Carrying this motto into her adulthood, Mary Kay became known as the most successful female entrepreneur in America. In fact, many say it was against all odds that she began her cosmetic company in 1963, which continues to flourish today.

"My Mary"

While my father was irresponsible in caring for his family and was not home much of the time, when he was home, he and I often played cards together. No surprise there, right? We played Go Fish, War, and even an occasional game of Blackjack. I cherished those moments, of course. I was doing something with my dad. Other times, he'd nestle me under one arm while we worked together on the crossword puzzle in the newspaper. With just enough hints, even at an early age, I guessed a few of the words.

During those intimate times, Dad called me "My Mary." To this day, I know that because of Dad's positive words to me in my early childhood and his many kindnesses over the years, I see God, our heavenly Father, as loving and caring and kind. I see Him as my Abba (Daddy) Father (Mark 14:36). There are times I even imagine the Lord calling me "My Mary." After all, it says in His Word that He calls His sheep by name (John 10:3). When I hear those words in my spirit, I am comforted, reassured, and encouraged in my faith—and I'm reminded of my earthly father and the precious and few times we spent together.

Besides my dad, many in my youth influenced me with their affirmative words. If you recall a relative, friend, teacher, mentor, or coach who encouraged you and spoke positively into your life, think about writing a note of thanks to them. On the flip side, make a point often to write, call, or visit others and speak life-giving words to them, keeping in mind that what you say to others today could influence them for years to come, maybe for the rest of their lives.

To those who have been on the receiving end of negativity and may be walking around with one or two unhealthy childhood mottos, there is hope, which we will begin to uncover in the next chapter. I guarantee, if you have a heart open to understanding and are willing to take time to consider why those words were spoken to you in the first place, you can begin to heal and walk in the freedom God has for you.

it's **your** turn

1. What words spoken to you as a child do you believe became a positive or negative childhood motto? Maybe you have more than one motto. Feel free to list them here.

2. If the motto was positive, how has it affected your life over the years?

3. If the motto was negative, what has been its effect on you?

4. Who in your life today could benefit from hearing your positive words of affirmation and encouragement? Make a list and then make a point to call or write.

2

seeing the words
for what they really are

Whatever you are overflowing with will spill out when you are bumped.

INDIAN PROVERB

In chapter 1, we looked at words that have left indelible marks on the hearts, minds, and souls of those to whom those words were directed. Many of those marks have become lingering wounds and scars, some of which may never heal.

Some men and women will carry those wounds their entire lives, like Olivia, who was told she was homely, and Marilyn, who wasn't granted the playground swing. Many never come to terms with the effects words have had on them or know that freedom from those words is available. Others will allow the effects of the words to justify their actions, blaming someone else for why they are the way they are or why they do the things they do.

Thankfully, there will be those who see the words for what they are, most often evidence of brokenness and hurt in the person who issued them. And this is what I offer as the first step in being set free, once and for all, from our prison of words. You see, it is inevitable that hurt people, those with broken hearts, will hurt other people. Recall that out of the abundance of the heart the mouth speaks (Luke 6:45). So if a heart is broken, and many of our hearts are at various degrees of brokenness, how can we *not* issue cruel and spiteful words? Our level of brokenness will determine just how hurtful our words will be.

Do you recall from chapter 1 some of the words spoken to me? I can guarantee my mother did not get up each morning and plan to wound me with her words. Of course, she didn't. She loved me. She worked hard to care for my little sister and me when there was next to nothing to work with in the way of finances. She sewed us beautiful clothes, cooked us nutritious meals, and made sure we got to take part in church and school functions, proud of us when we did. But Mom was extremely hurt. She had a broken heart. It's no wonder, then, that what came out of her mouth at times were hurtful, negative, and stinging words and that most often they were directed to the ones she loved the most, her two daughters.

Mom's Story

When Mom was nine months old, her mother died. She was four years old when her father died. Mom and her two older brothers went to live with their aunt and uncle, who became "Ma" and "Pa" to her and the only grandparents I ever really knew. Grandma and Grandpa Essa merely added three more children to their four, so Mom grew up one of seven children, many of those years during the Great Depression.

Before I go further in Mom's story, is it any wonder one of my childhood mottos was "If you can't eat it, don't buy it"? Mom remembered Depression-era food lines and coupons for commodities. Resources were scarce—and treasured. Food was carefully divvied out—and appreciated. Throughout Mom's growing-up years, not much was left from Grandpa's weekly factory check after their mortgage payment, putting food on the table, and what was required to run their household. The kids even shared their chewing gum. Okay, that was probably too much information.

I remember Mom telling me about being in high school and nightly washing out her one and only pullover sweater, a gift from one of her brothers who entered the workforce upon high school graduation. Clothes were not a luxury back then; they were a necessity. Interestingly, the family's address was on Easy Street. There was nothing easy about their lives, for sure. But Mom also shared good memories of growing up, always appreciative of what Grandma and Grandpa did for her and her brothers.

So the words "If you can't eat it, don't buy it," which for a period of time caused me undue anxiety, were justifiably founded. I believe Mom's experience of living during the Depression years also contributed to her telling her little girls not to ask for anything and to refuse something when offered when we visited family and friends. She grew up with little, and so did those in her community. Could it be that out of consideration for them, she didn't want to take from their cupboards?

Daggers to Mom's Heart

When Mom was old enough to ask questions about her own mother and father, she was told her dad was abusive to her mother. When Mom (baby Catherine) was still in her mother's womb, her father physically battered his wife, which may have contributed to her early death. This news was like a dagger to Mom's young heart. She told me once that from that point on, she blamed her father for her mother's premature death. Mom's already broken heart became even more shattered, except now resentment was added to the mix.

In her early twenties, Mom met my father one summer afternoon at a church picnic. This black-haired, attractive, young Assyrian man swept Mom off her feet, and they soon married. Dad's gambling habits had long been established, so his addiction showed up early. I entered the world in their first year together. My sister was born seven years later. From nearly day one of their marriage, a battle raged. When Dad said he played cards or went to the racetrack on Friday nights in order to make more money for his family, Mom would reply, "If you'll just come home with your pay, we can have everything we need!" Dad coming home right after work on Fridays rarely happened.

Thankfully, Mom had a strong constitution. She was tiny but a woman of colossal inner strength. At her tallest, she was four feet eleven, but God made her feisty and steadfast. For seventeen years, Mom did all she could to make her marriage work and hold together her fractured family.

Mom stayed, but she was not happy. In fact, Mom was extremely unhappy; she was angry, she was bitter, and she was hurt. As was emphasized in chapter 1, hurt people hurt other people. My sister and I got our share of spankings, but even worse were the words that came at us. Mostly, they were undeserved words, words that cut deep.

Speaking for myself, while a few of those words linger today and from time to time rear their ugly heads, I have dealt with most of them, seeing them for what they were. I know now they were *not about me*. None of them were. And they were *not about my sister*. They were solely reflective of Mom's brokenness.

The words were said out of anger, frustration, hopelessness, and despair. But what do children know? What skills do youngsters have to separate the words from the emotions and immediate circumstances behind them? Instead, we take them in and tuck them away in our minds and hearts.

My Aha Moment

When I began to see that the harsh words spoken to me in my formative years were not about me, I started seeing everything differently. Remember, out of the abundance of the heart the mouth speaks. The harsh words coming forth from Mom's mouth reflected what was going on in her heart. Frankly, at times, Mom was just too broken to speak anything but hurtful words. Her actions often spoke otherwise, but her words stung.

Here's where life gets a little more complicated. You see, Mom's words only served to exacerbate a heart already breaking—mine. Mom saw the shortcomings of her husband, and I saw the neglect of a father to his wife and young daughters. I watched other dads care for and spend time with their families, and I longed for the same. I watched kids run out to greet their dads coming home from work, families going on vacations together, parents and children worshiping together.

Were it not for the Lord, who came to heal the broken-hearted (Ps. 147:3), I too and perhaps many of you might be spewing words of wrath to those around us. We could all be walking around with perpetually damaged hearts, passing down to the next generation our legacy of brokenness.

What about Olivia and Marilyn?

With my new understanding, I considered little Olivia, who was told by her older sister that she was homely. Is it possible the sister's words had nothing at all to do with Olivia, that what was said came from someone with a broken heart, a teen who had to give up her adolescence much too soon to care for her ailing mother, as well as her younger siblings? I put myself in her shoes and thought about how I might feel if I had to take over running the household, cleaning, cooking, and was no longer free to spend time with my friends. She may even have had to prematurely quit school when she exchanged her role as teenage daughter for homemaker and surrogate mother, which could leave someone hurt and brokenhearted—even angry and resentful.

Since little Olivia was too young to correctly process her sister's words, and probably had her own wounded heart because of her mother's debilitating illness, she took in the words that said she was homely and believed them. Then she carried them around her entire life. And quite possibly, in fact, if I were a betting person like my dad was, I would wager that the words of Olivia's sister had absolutely nothing to do with Olivia but everything to do with the hurt her sister carried in her own heart.

I thought about young Marilyn too when she was told she couldn't have the swing out on that playground. Who knows what was going on in the heart of the little girl who said those words for everyone to hear? Sometimes kids just say nonsensical things. Or it might have been another child's name she called out, but she happened to look in Marilyn's direction. Only the Lord knows. The problem though is that young Marilyn, like Olivia, took the words into her heart and carried them with her for years.

How about Little Rich?

Farming is not an easy way to make a living. Most farmers will tell you that they and generations before them put blood, sweat, and tears into their work. Many labor from sunup to sundown, and depending on the type of farming, some cannot get away from their chores often or for any length of time.

It was natural for Rich Mullins's father to expect his son to follow in his footsteps. He most likely followed in his own father's footsteps, perhaps even inheriting his farm through his family. Rich was the oldest son, the one to whom the family farm would be handed down. Hopes and dreams were likely put into this elder son.

But Rich proved early on that farming did not come naturally to him. Music did. And this did not please his father in the slightest. Even as Rich successfully made his way through the music world, the movie about his life did not indicate his father ever said the words Rich naturally longed to hear. The words he heard as a boy echoed instead: "Everything you touch gets broken!" In the case of the broken machinery, it's understandable his father would be frustrated, discouraged, and upset about having to repair something so vital to his livelihood.

I wonder, were the words he spoke and the harshness he exhibited to his son a result of frustration and his own broken dreams of having his son follow in his footsteps, which quite obviously was not going to happen? Is it possible those negative, hurtful words directed at young Rich were not about the youngster at all but rather all about how the father was feeling when he spoke them?

And What about Lee?

We don't know all the issues in the relationship between Lee Strobel and his father. What we do know from the book and later the movie is that throughout the years, their relationship was rocky. It apparently came to a head the night before Lee's high school graduation when, after yet another argument, he left home for a summer job and didn't return for years.

At his father's funeral, Lee met several of his father's friends. They were all cordial to him, saying they were glad to finally put a face with his name. Apparently, over the years, throughout Lee's award-winning journalism career, his father displayed Lee's articles and boasted about his son.

Yes, Lee's father loved and admired his child. But his communication skills were lacking. There also may have been some pride, maybe even a little shame, that prevented this father from ever letting his son know his true feelings. Instead, the words that lingered in Lee's subconscious were that his father didn't have enough love for his son to fit into his little finger, which could very well have been a factor that helped nudge him onto the pathway of atheism.

Following his wife's conversion to Christianity, Lee likely added increased cynicism to his already staunch conviction that there is no God and struck out to prove he was right—only to prove himself wrong. Thus, he was converted to Christianity, which led to the book and movie *The Case for Christ*, now monumental Christian resources.

It would be safe to say that the words spoken by Lee's father were not about Lee but rather were said out of anger and frustration, perhaps even from never feeling loved by his own father.

Oh, if so many of us could go back and live life again. But that's hindsight, isn't it? We don't get to go back, but I hope we learn from our experiences and the experiences of others.

Sticks and Stones

How many times, at least in my generation, did we hear the adage "Sticks and stones may break my bones, but words will never hurt me"? We see now that while we used those words to try to steel ourselves from the demeaning words others said to or about us (now we call it bullying), those words are powerful. And in most cases, perhaps the sticks and stones would have been better, for wounds inflicted by sticks and stones heal much quicker and more easily than those received from mean and spiteful words. Wounds inflicted by sticks and stones often become badges of honor. Hurtful words, on the other hand, only serve to perpetuate and aggravate an already broken heart.

Now What?

If you've had hurtful words spoken to you, words that have become mottos, words you still may be carrying, words that affect your thoughts and actions, and you now have an insight as to why they may have been spoken, what do you do?

First, determine in your heart to see the words for what they truly are or were. When possible, be willing to discover the other person's story. You may already know it. If so, ask the Lord to reveal truth and to show you their broken heart. I can tell you from experience that when God showed me the condition of Mom's heart from all she had experienced from her early life on, I began to love her in a different way.

Instead of resentment, I felt sorrow for all she had been through. Instead of anger, I had compassion for her. I was able to extend grace and mercy, and to pray the Lord would bring her healing and finally mend her broken heart. I'm not sure that happened before she went home to be with Him. In her final years, she was diagnosed with dementia. Was it a blessing in disguise, perhaps God's way of removing those moments from her memory, bringing her the peace she so deserved?

Second, begin the process of choosing to forgive, which we will talk more about in the next chapter. Many say forgiveness is a process, meaning it doesn't happen all at once although it could. When we do come to the point of extending forgiveness, it may be best to go to the person, if possible, especially if spoken words caused a breach in the relationship. Or it may be best to merely spend some time with the Lord and extend forgiveness in prayer, never bringing up the matter to the one who spoke the hurtful words. In my case, I never wanted to bring any of this to Mom's attention; it would have only hurt her more. I just forgave her, loved her with a new kind of love, and got on with my life.

Also, keep in mind, forgiveness does not mean you need to continue to be the brunt of someone's hurtfulness. It will be up to them to get healing for their heart, which is something only the Lord can help them do. Your forgiving them does not give them license to continue to abuse you with their harmful words.

Remember too, this is all a process—first choosing to understand someone's story and then choosing to forgive them. Even after that happens, it may still take time to get over the effects of those words. After all these years, I continue to have issues when I walk into a department store. Often, I've had to take a few moments and remind myself that while I may not be able to eat my purchase, it's okay for me to shop. That's a little to the extreme, but that's how long some effects can linger.

What If You Don't Know Their Story?

Following is an example of someone being able to look behind words. It's from author and conference speaker Wendy Walters and her Facebook post titled "What's really going on here?"

This morning we had a call in the office that was like a violent attack . . . we literally felt the words in our physiology.

It was shocking, and really took us quite off guard. My assistant was supremely professional and handled the situation well, and when we got just a little past the episode, I began to think about what was really behind it. I was suddenly overwhelmed with compassion, knowing that behind that call was desperation, misdirected anger, and a deep hopelessness. They were lashing out at anything they may possibly be able to exert some control over as a reaction to all the giant impossibilities for which they feel held captive. I've been there.

Wherever you encounter people, know that there is a long story of which you are not aware. It doesn't excuse inappropriate behavior, but knowing you don't know the whole picture allows you to exercise grace and respond with compassion beyond your own nature or ability.

Character is revealed in these moments if you will allow awareness to translate to application. I think we all have opportunities to say, "There but for the grace of God . . ." and dig a little deeper to go the extra mile.[1]

There will be times we know a person's story and what's going on behind their words. When we don't though, we can trust what Scripture tells us, that words are true reflections of a person's heart. And if so, then we can offer understanding and compassion, and we can pray God will heal their brokenness.

We introduced this chapter with an Indian proverb: "Whatever you are overflowing with will spill out when you are bumped." In other words, your true character will show in your actions—and words—when you are under pressure. We are under no greater pressure than when we walk around with bruised and broken hearts. Keep that in mind when someone's words feel cruel and spiteful. Most likely those words are not at all about you.

it's **your** turn

1. From your list in chapter 1, take one of the child-hood (or adulthood) mottos and list it here along with the name of the person who issued those words to you.

2. To the best of your knowledge, how would you recap that person's story?

3. List from that person's story reasons why they may have said those words to you.

4. If you are able to see that person in a different light, now that you have a better understanding of why the words may have been spoken, write out how and why.

3

choosing to forgive

Forgiveness is the key that unlocks the door of resentment
and the handcuffs of hatred. It is a power that breaks the
chains of bitterness and the shackles of selfishness.

CORRIE TEN BOOM

When I sat down at my computer to begin this chapter, I wondered what more could be written on the immense topic of forgiveness. My search on the leading online bookstore found some 34,000 books with the word *forgiveness* somewhere in their titles. There will be even more by the time you're reading this chapter.

What freshness could I bring to this enormously important topic? Paramount in the Christian faith, the concept of forgiveness is crucial to grab ahold of for those of us desiring to attain a level of wholeness and healing in whatever area we are struggling.

Before we jump into this great expanse, let's recap. In chapter 1, we explored how words spoken to us early in life, or even yesterday, tend to influence us throughout our lives—some positively but far too many negatively. In chapter 2, we discussed possibilities for why harmful words were spoken and what may have been behind them. And we stressed that often the words are not about us but about what's going on in the hearts of those speaking. In many cases, we find broken hearts filled with bitterness and resentment.

If what we discussed in the first two chapters resonates with you and if the questions at the end of those chapters point to something specific in your life, then more than likely you are ready to consider the next step toward healing and freedom, which is choosing to forgive.

In the event, however, you need more proof that harsh words and actions emanate from a broken heart, let me share one more story with you before we move on to discuss what it means to forgive.

Another Thrift Store Find

Consider the story of Stormie Omartian, who began her writing and speaking ministry in 1997 with her first book, *The Power of a Praying Wife.* Her autobiography, titled *Stormie,* caught my eye one day while scanning the shelves at our local Habitat for Humanity ReStore.

Stormie's book turned out to be the first title I pulled from my bag of treasures when I got home. I read it cover to cover in two sittings, mining the nuggets of gold I soon realized would reinforce this chapter.

Briefly, Stormie's mother had mental issues and exhibited two distinct personalities, one for company and one for her immediate family, which for many years consisted of her husband and only child, Stormie. From the time Stormie was three years old, she remembers frequently being locked in a small closet beneath the stairway of their two-story farmhouse. On the first occasion, she had merely asked for a drink of water. "Get in the closet until I can stand to see your face!" her mother yelled in response to her daughter's simple request.[1]

As a little girl, Stormie could not understand why her mother, Virginia, was always angry. She abused her in other ways too, but what stuck with Stormie for many years and eroded what little self-esteem she could muster throughout her teen years and young adult life were her mother's demeaning, accusatory, and hateful words.

Well into her adulthood and after counseling for severe depression, Stormie traveled to her mother's hometown and spoke with her grandfather, as well as aunts and cousins, to try to understand the origin of her mother's hatred. Family members shared that young Virginia, the middle child of three daughters, was beautiful and well liked but also stubborn, lazy, and obstinate.

Outgoing and congenial at social gatherings, at home she was often cruel and cold. When Virginia was eleven, she had a heated argument with her then nine-month-pregnant mother, who went into labor a few hours later. That same night, both mother and baby died.

Did Virginia see these deaths as both a punishment and rejection? Did they leave uncensored guilt and unbearable grief, which in turn led to deep emotional scarring? No doubt, Virginia's heart was broken at a young and impression-able age and at a time in history when the kind of therapeutic help available today for healing was unheard of.

After her mother's death, Virginia's father was distraught; separately, the sisters entered foster care. A foster father Virginia came to love and admire died, adding more rejection and abandonment.

Stormie writes that after hearing this about her mother, she began to feel sorry for her. "She was someone to be pitied not hated."[2] While her new understanding did not excuse her mother, now Stormie could better comprehend what was behind her harsh words and actions.

Can you see that the words Stormie took into her own heart and mind were not about her but rather reflected her mother's broken heart and obvious mental illness? Once Stormie had more understanding, she was able to begin the process of forgiveness.

What Does It Mean to Forgive?

For our purposes, as forgiveness relates to the topic of the power of spoken words, we will examine what it might mean for those of us who have been the brunt of negativity and abuse. Before we do, let's look at how Merriam-Webster's dictionary defines the word *forgive*: "To stop feeling anger toward (someone who has done something wrong); to stop blaming (someone); to stop feeling anger about (something); to stop requiring payment of (money that is owed)." It appears, according to this definition, "to stop" is a common denominator. To *stop* feeling anger; to *stop* blaming; to *stop* requiring payment.

To stop something means that at one time we must have started something. At some point, we began feeling hurt and angry over something said, or we began using what someone said to justify what we say or do, or we started requiring others to pay for what they said. Maybe all three.

Since the Bible has much to say about forgiveness, and since the Bible was primarily written in Hebrew and in Greek, I examined those definitions for the word *forgive*. I found these common words: *pardon, send away, let go, release, deliver, set at liberty*. If I couple these with what I learned about bringing something to a halt, then it appears that for me to forgive I need to not only stop holding someone accountable but also take a forward motion to pardon them and set them free.

Now, that's something to think about. I might not have a problem stopping something, but I'm also required to let my offender off the hook? But here is what happens when I make a choice to do both: it empowers me. It puts me in the driver's seat, so to speak. It puts me in a place of command or control. Rather than other people and their words controlling my thoughts, feelings, and actions, I now assume that responsibility.

In other words, I am now in control of how I'm going to feel or respond or react to another person's words. Finally, I am in control of the situation and not the other way around, which is how I lived for most of my life. From my earliest recollections, I felt as though I were at the mercy of others, others in places of authority over my life, others stronger in personality than me. Hence, I lived as a victim for far too long. Thankfully, all that has changed. I pray it will for you too if you currently find yourself in that role.

First Step

Knowing I'm in control is my first step, and I believe yours, in becoming victorious. When I choose to *stop* feeling anger toward someone or *stop* blaming someone for words that became embedded in my life from early childhood and well into my adult years, and when I choose to *release* the people who spoke those words, I am positioned in a place of power. I am now on top of the situation or circumstance and no longer under it.

While stopping something is a choice in the making, sometimes it takes time and baby steps to put a stop to the effects of something that may have been going on for weeks, months, even decades, doesn't it? Perhaps, but maybe not.

I want to explore the victim mentality a little later, but for now, let's look at why it's important we take seriously the admonition to "stop" and "let go."

Why It Is Important

There are some things I need to have broken down into bite-size pieces to receive a clearer understanding of what's expected of me, especially when I'm directed numerous times in the Scriptures to forgive. So I used a set of questions from my high school English class and, later, my newspaper days. These were made famous by journalist and poet Rudyard Kipling (1865–1936) to trigger ideas and solve problems, and he immortalized them in a poem that begins: "I keep six honest serving men, they taught me all I knew; I call them What and Where and When and How and Why and Who."[3]

We've come to know these "honest men" as the 5 Ws and H.

Who needs to forgive? You need to forgive—and so do I—those who have hurt or offended us.

What do we need to forgive? The wrongs or offenses against us.

Where do we forgive? Any area in which we have been offended.

When do we forgive? Anytime, but the sooner the better.

Why do we need to forgive? The Scriptures tell us to forgive.

How do we forgive? As God in Christ has forgiven us (Eph. 4:32).

Who and *What* are easy to comprehend. So are *Where* and *When.* I want to spend some time looking at *Why* and *How.*

The *Why*

First, we are to forgive because we are admonished in the Scriptures to do so. "Because I said so," our heavenly Father might say to us. His actual words are "Be kind to one another, tenderhearted, forgiving one another, as God in Christ forgave you" (Eph. 4:32 ESV) and "Put on then, as God's chosen ones, holy and beloved, compassionate hearts, kindness, humility, meekness, and patience, bearing with one another and, if one has a complaint against another, forgiving each other; as the Lord has forgiven you, so you also must forgive" (Col. 3:12–13 ESV).

Second, God, in His infinite mercy, knows that to become all we can be for His purposes and for His glory and to live relatively happy and peaceful lives, even physically healthier lives, we need to let go of offenses and move on to victorious living.

Over and over in the research for this book, I came across accounts in which the pardoning of offenses, big and small, has been the key in obtaining the freedom to move forward for those who forgive. How I wish I had the space to write some of these accounts in full detail. They are stories of extremely harsh treatment followed by forgiveness and redemption. And while I cannot go into too much detail, I think it's important to share bits and pieces from some of these accounts.

Louis Zamperini

Louis "Louie" Zamperini was a 1930s Olympic distance runner, a US prisoner-of-war survivor in World War II, and a Christian evangelist. You will be familiar with his story if you read the book *Unbroken*[4] or saw the movie by the same name.

Louie was horribly and unjustly tortured during his time in the Japanese prisoner-of-war camps. This took place after he and his B-24 bomber crew of thirteen crashed into the Pacific Ocean while on a mission to find the crew of a lost plane. Louie and two others survived the crash, leaving them adrift at sea on their lifeboat for forty-seven days.

When they finally reached land in the Marshall Islands, only Louie and one other remained alive. Immediately, the two men were captured by the Japanese Navy. This was in 1943. Until the end of the war in 1945, the two survivors were held in captivity, severely beaten, and inhumanely abused.

Postwar, Zamperini suffered nightmares about strangling his former captors. He began to drink heavily to try to forget his wartime experiences. Waking up one evening, he found himself strangling his wife.

But God had another plan. In 1949 at a Billy Graham evangelistic crusade in Los Angeles, Louie turned his life over to Christ and became a new man. His nightmares ceased, he no longer felt extreme anger, and he was able to forgive his captors. He visited many of the guards from his prisoner-of-war days to let them know he'd forgiven them. Some became Christians in response to his testimony. *Captured by Grace*[5] is a documentary film highlighting Louie's life as a new man in Christ and Christian evangelist.

Eva Moses Kor

Eva Moses Kor is a survivor of the Holocaust who, with her twin sister, Miriam, was used for human experimentation by Josef Mengele, a German officer and physician, also known as the Angel of Death. Both of her parents and two older sisters were murdered at the camp; only she and Miriam survived.

Ten months before World War II ended in 1945, SS soldiers rounded up the Moses family along with other Romanian Jews and transported them in train cars to Auschwitz, the largest network of concentration camps in Nazi Germany. Two members of the Moses family were nine-year-olds Eva and Miriam. Eva documents her time at the concentration camp and her years following that experience in the film *Forgiving Dr. Mengele*.

Upon the girls' arrival at the camp, soldiers recognized the sisters as twins and separated them from the rest of their family. Eva describes watching her mother being pulled in one direction by one soldier while another soldier dragged her and Miriam in another. Seeing her mother's outstretched arms toward her helpless girls is Eva's last memory of her parents alive.

Taken to a separate barracks, where corpses of little children were strewn on the floor, Eva and Miriam and other twins were cruelly and unbelievably experimented upon for the purposes of genetic research.

We will stop the narrative at this point. After all, the purpose of this book is about the lasting effects words can have on someone. By using Eva's example, however, and because we are talking about forgiveness, I hope what I've summarized in these brief paragraphs is so horrendous that seemingly it would be something no one in their right mind could, or would, even want to forgive.

But in her later years, Eva realized that just being free from the hands of the Nazis after World War II did not remove the pain she experienced in the concentration camp. Her wounds went deep. How could they not? Her resentment and hatred did too. And who would not feel this way after such treatment? In addition, Eva was aware that the rest of her family spent their last minutes in gas chambers, their huge smoking chimneys with glowing flames visible to her young eyes day and night.

Eva said she discovered the only way she could break free from her prison of pain was to forgive. "There may be other ways to heal, but I have found one way. Forgive your worst enemy. It will heal your soul and it will set you free."[6] So much more could be said here about Eva and the years subsequent to her youthful experience, but we must move on.

Kitty Chappell

Most of us will never feel the steel muzzle of our father's loaded gun pointed into our temples and hear, "One of these days I'm going to blow your head off. I'm sick and tired of your interfering."[7] These words were spoken to then high school senior Kitty Chappell when she returned home one evening from church to find her father beating her mother with his Colt 45.

When Kitty pushed between her parents to protect her mother, her father put the gun to Kitty's head. Years later, Kitty, now a successful writer and speaker, described this tragic scene and many others, as well as the process of her healing and of forgiving her father, in her book *Soaring Above the Ashes on the Wings of Forgiveness*.

For too long, Kitty, her two younger siblings, and her mother suffered at the hands—and mouth—of Kitty's father. The brutality I read about in Kitty's book seemed almost surreal; her father's wicked words and actions were at times hard to fathom. How this family survived as long as it did without someone dying is nothing short of miraculous.

Yet, at a certain time in her life, Kitty was able to forgive her father for everything he said and did to her and her family. Was it easy? How could it be? Did she even want to? For a long time, no, she did not. Did it come naturally? Absolutely not. Was forgiveness the result of a choice she made? Unequivocally, yes.

Weary from the burden she carried, she knew that to forgive her father and to be set free from her prison of resentment, even hatred, she would have to *want* to forgive him. She began to pray the Lord would give her the desire to forgive her father. Here are her words about when forgiveness finally came:

> I don't remember when it happened—weeks, maybe months later—but I will always remember how it happened. One day, like a gentle breeze blowing the sweet fragrance of honeysuckle blossoms through the still air of a moonlit night, a sudden desire to forgive my father enveloped me. The bitterness in my heart melted as I whispered, "I forgive you, Dad—for everything!"[8]

For Kitty, the cleansing tears of relief that followed washed away all the rancid remnants of resentment.

And Now the *How*

The answer to the *how* in our list is *as God in Christ has forgiven us.* And how did God do that? Through the substitutionary death on the cross of His Beloved Son, Jesus Christ, on our behalf. Over 2,000 years ago, God's sinless Son died for you and me. Thus, we have been forgiven, pardoned, and released from sins for which we should pay—but won't have to.

In His unconditional and all-encompassing love, God sent His Son to die once for all—that is, all people and all sins, past, present, and future. There are times I have a hard time wrapping my mind around a God so loving that He would pardon sins that are committed against Him daily, sins of commission and sins of omission, big sins and small sins committed by you and me. They are sins that blaspheme His name and cause hurt to those created in His image.

But His Word tells us He has made provision for us to be totally and unconditionally pardoned and set free. And that's hard to grasp—pardoned completely, totally, and without condition. That's forgiveness I, as a human being, have a hard time offering. But that's the kind of forgiveness He requires of us. Total and complete to others just as He in Christ forgave (and continues to forgive) you and me.

Not to be mistaken by definitions that talk about the paranormal, ghosts, the occult, and such, His forgiveness is supernatural. In its purest form, *supernatural* is "something attributed to some force beyond scientific understanding or laws of nature." It's the supernatural transforming of our hearts and minds by God that allows us to forgive others the way He forgives us.

Author and Christian counselor Tim Clinton writes:

> Forgiveness is often thought of as a Christian duty. Forgiveness can rarely be achieved when practiced as a duty, however. The positive, loving emotions of forgiveness that replace the delayed emotions of unforgiveness rarely flow from willful duty. Instead, they flow from a heart that is transformed by having experienced God's love and forgiveness.[9]

Listen, it's not natural for us to offer this kind of forgiveness, yet we are scripturally instructed to forgive. How do we do that? It's only by understanding how we are forgiven that we can forgive. It's only in realizing that on our own, we deserve the worst, but we get God's best. It's only in appreciating what has been done for us that we can turn around and want to release someone else from offenses they've committed against us.

And it's only in God's supernatural mending of our hearts and minds and giving us new eyes to see others the way He sees them, with love and compassion, that we are able to stop holding them accountable and let go of the offenses.

How could Stormie Omartian begin to feel compassion for her mother instead of bitterness? God was healing and transforming Stormie's heart as she learned of her mother's past.

How could Louie go back and minister to those who tortured him during World War II? When he encountered God at the crusade, Louie was saved and became a new man with a new heart and a new love for others, even those who horribly wronged him.

How could Eva return and show understanding and grace to her captors? God gave her eyes to see that to be completely free of her gruesome experience, she would need to make a decision to extend forgiveness to her enemies.

How could Kitty release her father from the effects of his abusive treatment of her and her family? She surrendered her will to the Lord and asked Him to help her want to forgive her father.

In each case, God's supernatural love and power became theirs, enabling them to extend forgiveness and move on.

The answer to our *how* question is, then, in the same way that the Lord forgives us. His forgiveness is once and for all. Hebrews 7:27 says, "He sacrificed for their sins once for all when he offered himself." It's for the remission of my sins both past and present. And it's for any future sin I commit. Do I totally understand this? Does it matter if I understand it all? This is what I know: He loves me that much . . . and He loves you that much too. And He wants us to live in total freedom.

Jesus said He came to set the captors free. But too many of us remain incarcerated because we don't understand and aren't willing to receive the fullness of His love. Also, because we live in our own little reality shows where the rubber meets the road and we interact with other people, we tend to become offended.

For example, in a Bible study years ago, using Cynthia Heald's *Becoming a Woman of Excellence*,[10] I declared one day, "I *am* a woman of excellence." And then I added, "When it's just me and the Lord." My point was that in my quiet place, when it's just my heavenly Father and me, all is well. But problems, hurts, and offenses arise when other people enter the picture, people I need to forgive even if I don't want to or don't think I can.

So Why Don't We Forgive?

There are many ways we justify not extending forgiveness. Here are a few:

1. Comfortable in our role as victim, many of us don't know any other way to live. Often thrust into that role at an early age, we become victims of our environments, especially when our families of origin are broken, dysfunctional, and/or abusive. As children, we have no tools to get and stay safe, so we learn to live in fear, lack, and dread. It's not our fault. It's not a choice we would necessarily make, but that's where

we find ourselves, and as such, we are dependent on others for our own well-being. When that well-being is jeopardized, we fall into the victim role and become casualties early in life.

We take on the poor-me mentality and we get stuck. And it's not easy to get unstuck, especially if we've spent many years in that role. Then, since we don't know any different, except by what we might observe in the lives of families who seem to have it more together than we do, we become comfortable in what we know. And we stay, some of us for far too long.

We might say something like, "At least I know what to expect." It's not that we like this role. But rather we think it's our lot in life, especially if we don't see a way out.

2. As long as we withhold our forgiveness, we feel our offender is being punished. The irony is, in a lot of cases, the other person isn't even aware of their offense and is doing just fine. We, on the other hand, are the ones unnecessarily penalized.

3. We simply cannot forget the offense. But Jesus never said to forget the offense; He said to forgive the offender. Too many of us equate forgive with forget. But our not being able to forget an offense does not eliminate our need to forgive. We might forget as time goes on, but that has nothing to do with whether we want to get and stay free.

4. We might think we'll never be able to trust that person not to commit the same offense, or another. We

are afraid to hope things could get better or be different. And we could be right, because when we place our hope and trust in other people, no matter the relationship, disappointment is inevitable.

We humans are fallible, fickle, and faulty. The only perfect One in whom we can place our hope and trust is God, our Creator, our promise keeper, our Redeemer, the lover of our souls, the One who always has our best interest in mind, and the One who will arrange the forces of the universe on our behalves.

5. We believe the act may require us to continue in a relationship with someone who has hurt us and with whom we feel defenseless. This is where knowing how to set healthy boundaries is so important, a topic we will discuss in chapter 6.

6. Sometimes we think our forgiveness will excuse someone's poor behavior. But that's not what forgiveness is about. We offer forgiveness to set ourselves free. Someone else's behavior is between them and God. We don't need to subject ourselves to further abuse, but to withhold forgiveness because we fear doing so will excuse poor behavior is just that—fear. And fear does not come from the Lord (2 Tim. 1:7).

7. The one who offended us has not asked to be forgiven. But we can't afford to wait. It's possible the person who offended us may not even realize it. They may have forgotten when harmful or spiteful words were spoken. In the extreme, the person who

hurt us with their words may no longer be alive. It's in our best interest to take steps to forgive, whether it has been requested or not.

8. Some of us merely don't know how to forgive. As I mentioned earlier in this chapter, forgiveness is a huge concept, especially if we do not feel forgiven. Spend time in God's Word. When Scripture reveals who you are prone to be, you can develop an appreciation for what He has done for you and then be desirous of extending that same kind of grace and forgiveness to others.

9. Finally, some of us refuse to forgive, choosing rather to hold on to resentment, bitterness, and even hatred. Our broken hearts have hardened, and we are content to live out our lives in that state. What an unhealthy and unhappy way to exist—for us and for those with whom we live and work. We will be the ones who spew, from our broken and hardened hearts, hurtful words to others. And, sadly, the legacy of verbal abuse will perpetuate.

In summary, forgiveness is about freedom—your freedom and mine. It's about making a deliberate choice to stop holding others accountable for words that have injured us, and it's about letting the offenders go, which, in turn, frees us from our prisons of words.

In the next chapter, we will discover what to expect once we've made the choice to forgive, and we'll attempt to dispel beliefs about ourselves based on the words of others. Instead, we'll replace their words with those of God, our Creator and advocate. Are you ready? I pray so. It will be so worth it—to forgive, that is, and to move on in the freedom God has for you.

Don't be a victim any longer. Don't be a prisoner any longer. Walk in the freedom many have found when they made the choice to extend forgiveness and move on in their newfound liberty.

it's **your** turn

1. After reading chapters 1 and 2 and the examples in this chapter, how do you feel about extending forgiveness to someone who may have abused you with their words?

2. List the steps you will take to extend your forgiveness.

3. If you're having difficulty extending forgiveness, in what category or categories do you find yourself in the list of reasons why we don't forgive?

4. What might you do to reach the point of wanting to extend forgiveness?

4

the truth about you

How brief is the instant of a snowflake . . . and yet how exquisitely it was formed for such momentary existence.

JOAN WALSH ANGLUND

If you've opened to this chapter after having made the choice to forgive, you've just made a courageous move. Choosing to extend forgiveness is not necessarily easy, but it's a major step in moving ahead to a happier and more fulfilling life. Let's look at what you might find on the other side of forgiveness.

You've Chosen to Forgive, But . . .

Once we've made the decision to forgive someone, we often still feel the same about ourselves. We may even say something like, "When I look in the mirror, I still see the person I was before. Why don't I feel any different about myself?"

For those who walk around with poor self-esteem and negative feelings about their worth based on words spoken to them in their childhood—or just the other day—realize that at a certain point after you took in the words of others, you began to believe them. "You're ugly," "You're disgusting," "You will never amount to anything." The negative power of those words entered your spirit and soul and became part of your makeup. But those words were lies that came from a heart of bitterness, hatred, and brokenness. They weren't about you, as we talked about in chapter 2.

When you don't hear enough affirmative words to counter the damaging words, the offensive words become embedded in your fiber. But even if you do hear a considerable amount of positive words, you will tend to focus on the negative. I remember hearing a radio pastor say that his parishioners can shower him with praise after a sermon, but let one of them voice a negative comment, and it's that comment he takes home with him. That's just the way some of us are.

If you were told you are ugly, disgusting, or will never amount to anything, when you look in the mirror, that's what you tend to see—someone ugly and disgusting and so on, especially if those words came from a parent or from someone you thought you could love and trust. And if you're like most of us and have lived with those words for a long time, then no matter your number of successes, the words are there, just waiting for opportune times to rear their ugly heads and remind you of who *they* say you are.

But are you who they say you are? Or are you someone else, someone more attractive, someone with a future and a hope, someone with a reason for being and living life to the fullest? God, our Creator, the One who loves you and me more than any human being can and ever will, says you are. But you might ask, Does He say it about everyone?

Yes, He created us all and He loves us all the same. He says in His Word that He so loved the world (that would be everyone in it—then, now, and in the future) that He gave His one and only Son that whoever believes in Him shall not die but have eternal life (John 3:16). There are numerous Scriptures about God's all-encompassing love. Please take time to look them up and write them out. Then keep them handy and read them often to remind yourself of His steadfast and abounding love.

You see, He not only created you, but He also fashioned you in His image. Every human being is created in the image of God (Gen. 1:27).

> It is precisely the Image of God that makes man *human*; man could not *lose* the Image without ceasing to be what he is. Furthermore, it is only because he retains it, even in a broken or distorted form, that man is *redeemable* and *worth redeeming*. Without it, God would have had no reason or motivation to send His Son to die on our behalf. This is a vital point, not only from a strictly theological point of view, but also in connection with practical issues, such as the sanctity of human life."[1]

We hear much about the sanctity of life, especially when it comes to the topic of choosing life over abortion. But sanctity of life refers to you and me as well. Once we are created in the image of God, then we are not only to value the life of the unborn but also to understand that the sanctity of life is a principle of implied protection of *all* lives. In His image we are holy, sacred, and of great value, and we are not to be violated in any way—not by someone's actions nor by their words.

God's Word Is True

Much of how we feel about ourselves depends on how we feel about the One who made us.

In case you believe you are here by the accident of someone's sperm colliding with someone's egg and your birth is by chance, let's see what the Bible says about your beginnings and mine.

Psalm 139 talks about how He created each one of us, knitting us together in the wombs of our mothers. And He did so with a plan in mind, a blueprint designed just for you and me. In that blueprint are our unique DNA, giftings, talents, one-of-a-kind personality styles, and distinctive features. Even if we were born an identical twin, studies show there are still inimitable differences. If we are to believe anything said about us, then we should believe the words of the One who made us.

To wrap our minds around what God has to say about us, we must believe that the Bible, the Word of God, is true. Unfortunately, many today are not familiar with the Scriptures. When someone says something demeaning, ugly, and accusatory to or about them, they have nothing to fall back on. They don't know enough of God's Word to counter the lies.

Ed Stetzer writes in an article titled "The Epidemic of Bible Illiteracy in Our Churches"[2] that research shows one in four people polled in 2014 did not read any book in the preceding twelve-month period. So as recent as just a few years ago, many Americans (including churchgoers) were not reading any book, much less the Bible. These are sobering statistics when it comes to Christians. How many claim to believe the Bible is God's Word but do not read it? If we don't read the Bible, chances are we don't know what's in it, which translates to a lack of biblical literacy and beyond that a lack of understanding of biblical doctrine. It appears that many are merely not interested in reading the Bible.

Also, it's popular in today's culture to say the Bible is a book of myths and stories that may or may not have happened. I'm not going into a long discussion about the validity of God's Word. There are many resources affirming the Bible is factual, as well as much evidence to back up the experts who make such claims. I'm going to let you do your own research, and there's plenty of it. Lee Strobel, whom we talked about in earlier chapters, has published many resources that support the Bible and its claims.

If you are not sure whether to believe the Bible is true, please do your homework and read what scholars have to say. Ignorance is no excuse for us to walk around in our prisons of words when, in fact, if we just take some time to explore truth, we can walk in the freedom God offers.

Give the Bible a Chance

I was writing one afternoon at a local coffee shop. Since only a half wall separated my table from that of two young men, it took all the concentration I could muster to keep my mind on my work and not on their conversation. At one point, however, I heard one of them say he had tried reading the Bible. Now my interest was piqued. He said he had started in Genesis and didn't get very far before he found some crazy stories and decided the Bible was both weird and salacious. The other noted he found the Bible to be full of myths and fairy tales.

Because I understand the Bible to be so much different, I wanted to tell them the accounts they read were a result of a fallen world and that God the Father had a plan to set things right. At an opportune time—only as I felt the Lord open the door and after I apologized for seemingly listening in on their conversation, I said, "Give the Bible a chance. Try reading the New Testament first. Then the Old Testament will begin to make better sense. Start with the Gospel of Mark or the book of 1 John."

Pointing upward, I continued, "And then ask its author to give you understanding." The receptive young men and I chatted for a few more moments, and then we smiled and parted ways.

And that's what I want to say to you. If you have tried reading the Bible, maybe starting with Genesis, but found yourself lost or overwhelmed by all the names and numbers—and yes, unusual stories—and then put it down or packed it away, give the Bible a chance and ask its author to give you understanding.

One of the Scriptures God gave me when I was a child is Matthew 7:7: "Ask, and it shall be given you; seek, and ye shall find; knock, and it shall be opened unto you" (KJV). I encourage you to do that very thing if you'd like to be able to understand the Bible. Ask Him today, right now, to give you understanding; seek after it with all your heart; knock on His door every morning and enter into His presence to receive His encouragement and the truth about who He says you are.

Take time to allow God to reveal Himself to you. Take time to quiet yourself and get into His presence, for when you're reading His Word, it's as though the two of you are sitting across from one another in one of your favorite spots and having an intimate conversation.

Will the Real You Please Stand Up?

There are many Scriptures that tell us who we really are, but for our purposes we are going to look at only a few.

God says in Psalm 139:14 that we are fearfully and wonderfully made. We are unique, one-of-a-kind living and breathing miracles. It has been said the human body is the most complex and unique organism in the world. Just imagine a newly conceived human life. From that one cell within the womb develop all the different tissues, organs, and systems, which amazingly all work together in a coordinated process. An example is the hole in the septum between the two ventricles in the heart of the newborn. This hole closes at exactly the right time during the birth process to allow for the oxygenation of the blood from the lungs, which does not occur while the baby is in the womb and receiving oxygen through the umbilical cord.

A look at the human brain shows its ability to learn, reason, and control functions of the body, such as heart rate, blood pressure, and breathing. We can walk, run, stand, and sit, all while concentrating on something else. I know, you're thinking that's where multitasking got its name. And these are just two examples of our miraculous bodies.

Recall the quote at the beginning of this chapter. Imagine a God who intricately forms each snowflake so that no two of them are alike. He has done the same in us. We are here for a brief time, yet we are fearfully and wonderfully made to carry out the plans and purposes He has for each one of us.

At one time, I organized a program called First Step for Girls. In one of my groups in Aztec, New Mexico, I presented a mosaic butterfly craft to six ten-year-old girls. I gave each of them a copied outline of a butterfly. The girls were to take tiny squares and triangles cut out of colored construction paper and glue them onto the butterfly wings. The exercise was to show how different each person is, since no two butterflies would end up looking alike.

Five of the six girls began to glue the various pieces of construction paper on their butterfly wings, and the differences began to show up immediately. The sixth girl, however, decided to color her butterfly wings with crayons. Wait, that's not what I planned. I tried to encourage her to do as the other girls were doing (to prove my point). She was not to be convinced. Tempted to stand my ground, I realized before I made a fool of myself that her desiring to use crayons was her way of showing her uniqueness—the very point of the butterfly exercise. The teacher was taught a lesson that evening.

From time to time, the Prager University five-minute videos show up on my Facebook page. Recently, I watched the segment titled "The Missing Tile Syndrome."[3] Dennis Prager talks about the tile ceiling with one tile missing. Look up at the ceiling and what do we see? The place where the missing tile should be, of course. And this is generally where we place our focus, not on what is there but on what is not there.

Prager tells about his bald friend who enters a room and all he sees is hair. He talks about the petite woman who walks into a room and sees only the long legs of other women. He uses these examples to show us that we tend to focus on what we don't have rather than what we do. We see our flaws and focus on them instead of our strengths. We see what we do not have and zero in on what we desire.

This short Prager video reminds us it's okay to desire what we don't have but that we shouldn't spend a lot of time focusing on what's missing in our lives. We all have traits others would like to have but don't; it works both ways. Let's not get carried away by the Missing Tile Syndrome; let's learn from it and celebrate what makes you the unique creation you are and me the one-of-a-kind that I am.

Bought with a Price

The words "you're worthless" may be ringing in your ears. The Bible, however, says you are extremely valuable. It says you were bought with a price (1 Cor. 6:20) and that price was the ultimate sacrifice of God's Son.

"But I don't feel valuable," you might be saying. After all, look at the devaluing words you've heard about yourself. But God in His infinite love paid a great price for you. You are a magnificent work of art, and no one is to trample your value.

When words from the past ring in your ears, telling you you're worthless, counter those words with the Word of God, which says you were bought with a price, a price so high our finite minds have a difficult time comprehending just how much we are worth.

He Has a Plan

What else does God's Word say about you? He has a plan and purpose for your life. You are here for a reason, perhaps for many reasons. It's no accident you were born on the day you were born. He knew you before the foundation of the world (Eph. 1:4). He knew the day and the exact moment you would enter this world. And He knows the plans He has for you (Jer. 29:11).

So, we know from the source Himself that we are fearfully and wonderfully made, we are valuable because of what our lives cost Him, and we are gifted with plans and purposes for our lives. There is so much more you can find for yourself. Please don't rely on others to tell you these things. Today, there is no excuse for not being in the Bible. From book form to audio, and to our computers and smartphones, there is ample opportunity to read and hear God's Word!

The Choice Is Yours

I might step on some toes, but this is important to say. If you want to keep that miraculous brain of yours in good working order and your soul and spirit in good condition, you need to be mindful of what you see with your eyes and hear with your ears.

What books and magazines are you reading? What websites do you visit? What are you viewing on TV, the big movie screen, the internet? What are you exposing yourself to on social media? With whom do you spend your time? You've heard it said, and I repeat, there's a battle out there raging for your soul and psyche. The enemy, Satan, wants you to remain in your prison of words. He wants you to believe you are ugly, worthless, an accident, hopeless, and of no use in this world.

He does not want you to believe what God says about you and will work overtime to discourage and demean you. But you can control all that. Remember, you are empowered to no longer be a victim but rather a victor. Therefore, be careful what you allow into your heart and soul.

You have the power to turn off the TV, internet, and social media, and you have the power to choose to be with people who will build you up and not tear you down. You have the choice to associate with those who believe in you and in themselves, who have enough self-respect to be able to re-spect you the way the miraculous you should be respected.

What are you allowing through the gate of your ears? Harsh and crude words from today's popular music? It's not just today's music. When I listen to tunes from my teen years, and the words roll off my tongue as I sing along, I'm dismayed at what I listened to and allowed into my soul. I used to say I don't really listen to the words, I just love the melody, yet the words ring out quite easily after all these years.

Am I saying not to listen to anything but hymns and music by today's Christian artists and those of the past? Of course not. But I believe you need to balance what the world has to offer with lyrics that lift you up and do not tear you—or others—down.

Again, the choice is ours. It always has been. But when we are young, influences enter in that are often out of our control. When I was young, great emphasis was placed on the big screen. On weekends, we often went to see Hollywood movies on both Saturday and Sunday. My favorite magazine was *Photoplay*. Sitting on my front porch, I longingly gazed at the movie stars throughout its pages, aspiring to follow in their footsteps. I loved the new rock 'n' roll music that came on the scene in the 1960s.

I'm grateful for the balance church and traveling gospel singers played in my life back then. And for the many Sunday mornings when Dad and I sat on the living room floor and played cards. Always in the background were the televangelists of the day. Gospel seeds were planted and watered on those mornings in both of our hearts.

Are you young and single? Make choices that will increase your knowledge of the truth about you.

Are you a parent? Be sure your home offers balance in what your children see and hear. Let them see you watching and listening to what is wholesome and positive.

Are you a grandparent? Remind your adult children and grandchildren of their value. Be a role model for them in what you see and hear.

Whose Words Will You Listen To?

Olivia's sister said to her, "You're homely." I believe God would say to Olivia, "You are My beautiful daughter, and I take delight in you!" (see Zeph. 3:17).

Marilyn's playground nemesis told her that anyone could have the swing but her. I believe God would tell Marilyn, "I own the cattle on a thousand hills, and all the earth is yours as an inheritance" (see Pss. 50:10; 2:8).

Rich Mullins's father accused his son of breaking everything he touched. I believe Rich's heavenly Father would say to him, "I made you in My likeness with the ability to create.

Move in your gift of music and heal what the world has broken" (see Gen. 1:27).

The father of Lee Strobel told his son he didn't have enough love for Lee to fill his little finger. I believe God the Father would tell Lee, "I love you so much that I gave My Son's entire body on your behalf" (see 1 John 2:2).

My mom told me I was just like my father. I believe God would say to me, "My Mary, you are made in *My* likeness. As My Son was the visible representation of Me, you be like Him. I created you to serve like He served, love like He loved, go where He went to heal the brokenhearted and set the captives free" (see Luke 4:18).

Maybe someone has said you're a mistake and they wish you'd never been born. My heart aches even now as I think about someone whose mother told her she wished she had flushed her down the toilet. Oh, how I long to wrap my arms around this woman and tell her, "Your heavenly Father says that all your days are written in His book, that you are fearfully and wonderfully made, that He knit you together in your mother's womb" (see Ps. 139:13–16). No, whoever you are, you are not a mistake!

Maybe someone told you that no one really cares about you. Your Creator would say to you, "My thoughts toward you are as countless as the sand on the seashore" (see Ps. 139:18).

Perhaps someone told you to leave and don't come back. God would say to you, "Come home, and I'll throw the biggest party heaven has ever seen" (see Luke 15:11–32).

Do you see the difference in the words of humans as opposed to those of our heavenly Father? How is it that people who purport to love us and want to be with us can use their tongues to issue such hurtful words?

We answered that question earlier in this book. Let me put it another way, this time using the words of Dr. Ray Pritchard of Keep Believing Ministries, who writes, "The tongue itself is never the problem. The tongue merely reflects what is in the heart."[4] Ah yes, another confirmation that hurt, broken-hearted people hurt other people. How many more ways can we say it? Their words are not about you but rather all about what's going on in their hearts when the words are spoken. That being the case, why do we take those words into our own hearts and believe them to be true about ourselves?

I pray that by the time you finish reading this book and have taken a serious look at the questions at the end of each chapter, you will come to routinely think—maybe even verbalize—that the hurtful words coming your way are not about you. In addition, may you come to a point where you automatically counteract those words with what you believe God would say about you in any given situation.

Please Take It Personally

Others might say, "Don't take it so personally." And that's probably good advice, because often we take personally what was not meant to be personal, and unfortunately, we are too easily offended. But there is something I urge you to take personally, and that is God's Word. Here's a simple way to do that.

When I read Scripture, I like to put my name in the place of whom the context is referring to. For example, Philippians 4:13 reads, "I can do everything through Christ, who gives me strength" (NLT). I change it to say, "*Mary* can do everything through Christ, who gives *Mary* strength."

The psalms are great for this exercise. I enjoy printing out a psalm and appropriately inserting my name. Then I read it back to myself out loud as a declaration, expounding on the words for my own understanding. Let's take Psalm 1:1–3 as an example.

> How blessed is *Mary* who does not walk in the
>   counsel of the wicked,
> Nor stand in the path of sinners,
> Nor sit in the seat of scoffers!
> But *Mary*'s delight is in the law of the LORD,
> And in His law *Mary* meditates day and night.
> *Mary* will be like a tree firmly planted by streams
>   of water,
> Which yields its fruit in its season
> And its leaf does not wither;
> And in whatever *Mary* does, *Mary* prospers.
>   (NASB)

I hope you'll give this a try. In fact, consider doing so right now. Put your name where mine is and read this portion of Scripture out loud.

Something else you should take personally is God's love for you. God's love, just like His forgiveness, is hard to fathom, primarily because we try to compare it to the love we offer to and receive from others. Unlike this kind of love, God's love is steadfast and unchanging; His love comforts us; His love is everlasting, unconditional, and broad beyond comprehension.

When my grandson Daniel was a little guy, I would stretch out my arms as wide as I could and say to him, "Daniel, I love you this much!" I then asked if he loved me that much.

"No," he teased. "Then how much do you love me?" I asked. He replied, "I love you all, all, all!" I couldn't ask for more than that.

Recently, my three-year-old granddaughter, Annabelle, asked me if I loved her. "Oh, yes, I love you!" I replied. I then asked her if she loved me. She answered, "I love you so, so, so, so much!" I think there were a few more "so's," but you get the picture.

Well, this is all well and good for you, Mary, you might be thinking. It's well and good for you too, because our God, the One who knit us together in our mothers' wombs, does not show favoritism (Acts 10:34). What He's done for me, He can—and will—do for you.

He Disciplines Those He Loves

Just as we want to hear the positive things about ourselves from God's Word, so too will the Lord bring revelation and correction when we spend time with Him. Be open to all He has for you. He loves you too much to leave you where you are and will move you forward in His plans as you allow Him to, pointing out your goodness as well as areas in which you need to grow. Second Timothy 3:16–17 tells us: "All Scripture is God-breathed and is useful for teaching, rebuking, correcting and training in righteousness, so that the servant of God may be thoroughly equipped for every good work."

Think of Him as you would a good parent, one who always has your best interest in mind. If you are doing something detrimental to your well-being, a good parent will call it to your attention and bring correction, and then will show you a better way.

Just as God's love is different from that of people's, so is His correction. While correction from others might sound accusatory and bring condemnation, God's correction will be done gently and with conviction. That's how you can tell the difference. "Therefore there is now no condemnation for those who are in Christ Jesus" (Rom. 8:1 NASB). And there is no condemnation when you reach out to the Lord with a repentant heart and a desire to walk in His ways.

Ask and You Shall Receive

What do you need? Love, direction, understanding, provision? Ask and it shall be given.

What are you looking for? Love, direction, understanding, provision? Seek and you shall find.

What doors are you trying to open? Those of love, direction, understanding, provision? Knock and the door will be opened to you.

"It's not that easy," you say? It couldn't be easier. We simply need to make the choice every day to get into God's Word and let God's Word get into us. It's called the renewing of our minds so that we can walk in step with Him and in what He has for us. And the more we get into His Word, the more comfortable we become—even if we think we have a missing tile or two.

"He Said It"

There's a story about a young soldier in the French Emperor Napoleon's army who intercepted the runaway horse carrying his beloved commander. Just in time, the young private saved the emperor from possible death. When things settled down, Napoleon glanced down and said, "Thank you, Captain."

The private looked up with a smile and asked, "Of what regiment, sir?"

"Of my guards," answered Napoleon.

Putting down his musket, he proceeded to join a group of officers nearby. One of them, a general, asked, "What is this insolent fellow doing here?"

"This insolent fellow," answered the soldier, "is a Captain of the Guards."

"You're insane," said the general. "Who told you that?"

"He said it," replied the soldier, pointing to the emperor.

"I was not aware of your promotion," said the general politely.[5]

To those around him, this young man was still a private, dressed in the coarse garb of a common soldier, but in the bold assertion of his dignity, he met the taunts of his comrades and all his superiors with three little words, "He said it!"

What has God said about you? Hold fast to who you are in Him. And if anyone disputes your uniqueness, your possibilities, and your position in Him, just point up and say, "He said it!"

it's **your** turn

1. Like the pastor we read about early in the chapter, think of a time when one negative word stood out above other more positive words said to or about you.

2. Would you say you currently spend time reading the Scriptures regularly, often, occasionally, or not much at all? If you feel you need to read the Bible more, list what you can do to get into God's Word more frequently.

3. What missing tiles do you believe you have? What can you do to turn your mind from what you don't have so that you can appreciate and celebrate what you do have? Now might be a good time to list your positive traits.

4. In whatever role you are in, what can you do to ensure that a good balance of what you see and hear is accomplished for you and those you love?

5

breaking free through the power of prayer

> We must begin to believe that God, in the mystery of prayer, has entrusted us with a force that can move the heavenly world and bring its power down to this earth.
>
> ANDREW MURRAY

If I was taken aback by the number of books available on the topic of forgiveness, I was even more so when I saw there are over 184,000 books with the word *prayer* somewhere in their titles. Truly, if someone wants to have a rich and vibrant prayer life, there is no reason not to. Besides the Bible, there are numerous resources on this topic.

While not to oversimplify something this important, I offer that prayer is simply having a conversation with

God, our heavenly Father, whether we're sitting, standing, kneeling, lying prostrate on the floor, propped up on our beds, or sitting in our prayer closets, in our cars, on the beach, or on our back porches. Prayer is listening and talking and then listening some more. It's being honest in our concerns, and it's expecting to hear what God has to say to us through His Word. It's taking the time to get quiet before Him and surrendering our wills to the One who created us and knows our thoughts before we utter a word (Ps. 94:11).

While reading this book, have you been reminded of words from your past that have affected your well-being and perhaps help to explain how and why you do the things you do or feel the way you feel? Have you explored the background for those words? Have you determined in your heart to stop allowing those words to affect you and let the person who spoke them off the hook? Do you recognize that what God says about you in Scripture is true? If so, then come with me on this exploration of the power of prayer to break any strongholds still remaining that threaten to keep you locked in your prison of words. I call this kind of declaration "replacement prayer."

The negative words spoken to you, whether out of ignorance, fear, anger, or even intended maliciousness, are powerful. But so are your words to break any power they might still have over you. Some of those negative words have created concrete monuments that stand as memorials to the times they were spoken. And those monuments must come down. You can do that through the power of your own words and through the power of prayer. Let's explore how.

A Curse Is a Real Thing

While I do not intend to go into great depth about the topic of curses, we need to see something vitally important if we want to break down the monuments that cause us to return to and perhaps wallow in our pasts. First, let's recognize that too often we think curses are something deliberately placed on others to cause them harm, even death.

Matthew 21, where Jesus teaches the parable of the fig tree, shows that curses can come about in a much more casual manner.

> Now in the morning, as He returned to the city, He was hungry. And seeing a fig tree by the road, He came to it and found nothing on it but leaves, and said to it, "Let no fruit grow on you ever again." Immediately the fig tree withered away.
>
> And when the disciples saw it, they marveled, saying, "How did the fig tree wither away so soon?"
>
> So Jesus answered and said to them, "Assuredly, I say to you, if you have faith and do not doubt, you will not only do what was done to the fig tree, but also if you say to this mountain, 'Be removed and be cast into the sea,' it will be done. And whatever things you ask in prayer, believing, you will receive." (vv. 18–22 NKJV)

One day, as I wrote out verse 22 as my Scripture lesson for the day ("And whatever things you ask in prayer, believing, you will receive"), I felt compelled to go back and read the entire passage again. This time, I started with the heading, which in my version of the Bible reads "Cursing of the Fig Tree."

When I reread the story, I was impressed by the fact that Jesus did not say to the fig tree, "I curse you, and therefore you shall never again bear fruit." He did not mention anything about a curse. He merely said, "Let no fruit grow on you ever again." I'd say those were relatively benign words. Shortly after, however, the tree withered. And Jesus told the disciples who were with Him that they too could use words in a powerful way. Since I'm one of His modern-day disciples, I take those words to apply to me as well.

Now, the chances of my talking to trees are not great, but I did wonder, *Is it possible that words I speak to someone, or words that have been spoken to me, could cause something inside to wither and die?* Perhaps a dream or a vision of my future or my confidence or any number of other things.

To take it a step further, is it possible I've cursed someone with my words or vice versa? Is it possible that words spoken to you have become like a curse in your life?

One of the definitions in the dictionary for the word *curse* is "To bring great evil upon; to be the cause of serious harm or unhappiness; to furnish with that which will be a cause of deep trouble; to afflict or injure grievously; to harass or torment."

It mortifies me to think that words I have spoken might be some kind of curse. What about words spoken to or about me?

James 3:10 says, "From the same mouth come both blessing and cursing. My brethren, these things ought not to be this way" (NASB). Does this mean that if my words are not blessing someone, they are cursing that person?

Sometimes I think it might be best not to say anything at all. I don't know about you, but when I'm reminded of all this, I want to be extremely careful about what comes out of my mouth. My words are powerful—and so are yours!

That said, what words still haunt you even though you've taken steps to forgive and move on? Make a note of them right now or in the very near future. Then go to God's Word and write down what He says about you in this regard. For example, if words that said you would never amount to anything are still etched in your mind and tend to hold you back from something you'd like to explore, go to Jeremiah 29:11, where the Lord tells His prophet Jeremiah that He (God) knows the plans He has for Jeremiah, plans to prosper him and not harm him, plans to give him a future and a hope.

Since God is no respecter of persons and since Scripture tells us that He is the same yesterday, today, and forever (Heb. 13:8), we can take the promise God made to Jeremiah and apply it to ourselves. You're now ready to pray in this manner: "Father God, today I break the power of the words that say I will never amount to anything and choose to believe what You say about me, that You know the plans You have for me, plans to prosper me and not harm me, plans to give me a future and a hope. In Jesus's name, amen!"

By the way, I love what the word *amen* means: "So be it!"

Make a deliberate choice to focus on this portion of Scripture. Keep it close and stand on God's promise to you. No one else has the power to do this for you, but you have great power, with God's help, to do it for yourself. When you declare God's words over yourself, the power of the negative words is broken; the only way those words can have any hold on you again is if you choose to allow them to do so. The proverbial ball is now in your court.

Walk in Belief and Faith

Does this seem too simplistic? Hold on, there's more. This is where faith comes in. Now you need to walk in the faith that you have God's promise. A great lesson I took from my direct-sales days is the adage "Act the way you want to become, and you'll become the way you act." In other words, if God's promise to you is Jeremiah 29:11—which it most certainly is—take the necessary steps of faith to become successful in what you do.

Maybe like Olivia you were told you were homely. Pray against those words and appropriate God's words that say you are fearfully and wonderfully made. You might add Proverbs 3:15, which says, "She is more precious than jewels; and nothing you desire compares with her" (NASB). Now act beautiful! Not haughty and conceited, but rather walk in the kind of beauty God sees as He looks at His workmanship and says, "It is good."

Pray, "Father God, today I break the power of the words that say I am homely and choose to believe what You say about me, that I am fearfully and wonderfully made and that I am more precious than jewels. In Jesus's name, amen!"

By faith, now see yourself as the beautiful creation He made you to be. There is no one else in the world just like you. You are His one-of-a-kind masterpiece, created in His image. Will you have to remind yourself from time to time of the new you? Of course. At times, we get tired and weary, we get ornery, and we get discouraged from the cares of the day, and as a result we might be tempted to revert to old thinking. But remember, the ball is now in your court. Will you hold on to your promise and walk in the light of His words about you, or will you hit it back into the darkness of lies? It's totally up to you.

Here's a real caution as you pray against what was spoken and then appropriate what God says about you. As you rehash the words etched in your mind and heart, it's quite possible you will be tempted to once again assign the debt you've already forgiven to your offender.

I want to remind you that just as God in Christ has forgiven you, once forgiven, you are forgiven. He does not dredge up your past and hold it against you. He does not remind you of the sins you've committed. Therefore, do not allow yourself to dredge up the sins of others.

I can't stress enough that this is about your free will and the choices you have in life. Don't choose to be incarcerated once again. Just as you used the key to unlock your prison door, use that key again to lock the door with you on the outside. Throw the key away if you must, but do not go back to jail.

If you've ever played the game Monopoly, you are familiar with the admonition "Go to jail. Go directly to jail. Do not pass GO. Do not collect $200." In this case, I'm telling you to pass up the opportunity to once again cast blame on your offender and put yourself back in jail. Rather, *do* pass GO. *Do* pick up your $200—and every other good thing God has for you in this life. Friends, life on planet Earth is short. Stay out of jail. It's within your power to do so. So be it!

"He'll Never Change"

My mom often said of my dad, "He'll never change." And he didn't, in the way she wanted him to. Were her words holding him back from being the man he was created to be? Of course, these words were spoken from Mom's broken heart, her disappointments, her bitterness. Deep down she loved my dad. She wanted their life together to be different. She tried for a long time to make it work. But I wonder, *If she and others had spoken different kinds of words, life-giving words, to and about him, would he have been encouraged to get off the self-defeating track he was on and get on one more positive, more family building?*

If someone had believed in him and spoken words of life to him, would he have changed? Of course, now we will never know. He died at the age of fifty-three from lung cancer. Today, as I write this chapter, were he still alive he would celebrate his ninety-sixth birthday.

I can tell you this about my dad. He was a man for the people. His historic idol was Abraham Lincoln. He appreciated the work of Dr. Martin Luther King Jr., often playing the song associated with Dr. King's work, "We Shall Overcome." Dad ran for public office, wanting to represent the constituents of his community. He wrote songs and strummed the guitar; he even recorded a 45-rpm record prior to his too-early death. I believe he had greatness in him. I also know a little bit of his backstory.

Dad came from a family of six boys and one girl. He was born midway among the boys. Lastly, his mom had a baby girl. Today, we would attribute his mom's, my grandmother's, mental issues to postpartum depression, but back then they committed Dad's mom to a mental hospital, where she eventually took her life. Before she entered the hospital, she requested that her neighbors take her baby girl, leaving the six sons to be cared for by their father.

Following my grandmother's death, Grandpa married a woman with nine children. So for a time, there were fifteen kids growing up under one roof when times were not prosperous. Surely, those were not easy years. Theoretically, a child or two might well have fallen through the cracks. Naturally, a little brokenness to young hearts could be expected. Dad lost his mother when he was only nine. And the boys lost their baby sister at the same time. No grief counseling was available back then for Grandpa or his sons. They just sucked it up and went on with life. Dad's beginnings were rocky, to say the least.

There might have been a mentor or two in Dad's young life who encouraged him to be an achiever, and he must have been astute enough in history class to admire President Lincoln and his platform. But something else got ahold of him and turned his head to gambling and all its entrapments.

He wanted to help overcome injustices against others, but he was not able to overcome his own demons. He was in a prison of his own making, and the words "He'll never change" did nothing to help him break free.

I'm grateful to say that Dad was finally released from his prison, and before he died, he gave his broken heart to the Lord. I have the assurance that he's in heaven and that one day I will see him again, no longer ravaged by the effects of a hard life and cancer but a man in his new body. Instead of playing cards together, Dad and I will stand side by side before the throne of God and serve Him day and night. Mom and other family members will be there too. What a beautiful reunion that will be. No more hurtful words—only words of praise to our God and King!

Awakened by a Little Brochure

Are you praying God's Word over your life? If so, that's great. You will not be sorry as you break the power of negative words and replace them with His truth about you. If you're not praying God's Word over your life, what's stopping you, besides your own will and determination not to?

You say you are not comfortable enough with the Bible to know how to pray and break the power of negative words in your life? I understand. It took me a while to get familiar with the Scriptures. But once I had the desire to do so, it's as though God placed every opportunity in front of me to become acquainted with His "love letter" to me.

I remember a day in May of 1984 like it was yesterday. Sitting in my living room, going through the mail, I opened an envelope with a brochure inside titled "Born Again People." For some time, I had been on a spiritual quest, wondering what it meant to be born again. I was a little stunned to see my answer arrive in the mail.

At the end of the brochure were words we sometimes refer to as the sinner's prayer. It went something like this: "God, I know I am a sinner and deserve the consequences for my sin. Thank You for Your Son, Jesus, who took my sins upon Himself and died in my place. Thank You for forgiving me and saving me. In Jesus's name, amen."

As I read those words, I recognized them as being similar to the words prayed at the end of every Sunday morning program I watched all those many years ago with my dad. I repeated them as a little girl, and I said them again that day on my sofa. As I repented of my sins and accepted God's grace and mercy, I thought about my three children and all the years I had wasted.

Suffice it to say, in His perfect timing, He drew my daughter and both my sons to Himself, and He provided me an education I could never have imagined. The month after what I like to call my awakening, we moved from our home in Michigan to Ventura, California, where God placed our family in a Bible-believing-and-preaching church. Shortly after that, I was hired by a Christian publishing company where it was my job to listen to teaching tapes of pastors, teachers, and leaders in the faith. I took notes on everything I listened to and filed them away for future reference. God supplied me with learning I could not have accomplished any other way in such a short period of time.

A passage of Scripture says that God will restore the years the locusts have eaten (Joel 2:25). It truly came to pass for me and my children. If you feel as if you've wasted a lot of time in things that have no eternal value, look to God. He will do the same for you. He might not give you a job listening to Christian speakers, but He will supply unique-to-you opportunities to learn of Him. Once again, our God is no respecter of persons, and He has no favorites. Although sometimes when I think about how active He is in my life, I wonder how He has time for anyone else! But then, He is omniscient (all knowing), omnipresent (ever present), and omnipotent (all powerful). And this same God desires to have a relationship with you and me. Isn't that amazing!

Another teaching tool God had for me was a pastor who taught *from* the Bible, not *about* the Bible. He taught verse by verse, which is called *expository* or *exegetical* teaching. In other words, he explained the text. And he taught *contextually*, which means he taught the interrelated conditions in which events occurred. Sitting in that pew, I often felt like I was in Bible college. And for that I am eternally grateful.

My generous heavenly Father did not stop with Bible-college-like teaching. At that first Bible-believing-and-preaching church, He also provided me a tiny pamphlet titled *Where Do I Look for My Help from God?* Since I had little Bible knowledge at the time, this proved to be a very handy reference. Nowadays, it's easy to go online and find Bible helps. Here's a sampling of what I found when I did a quick Google search on the following topics:

For the more abundant life: "If you remain in me and I in you, you will bear much fruit" (John 15:5).

For needed help and strength: "So do not fear, for I am with you; do not be dismayed, for I am your God. I will strengthen you and help you; I will uphold you with my righteous right hand" (Isa. 41:10).

When confused and upset: "And the fruit of righteousness shall be peace; and the effect of righteousness quietness and assurance for ever" (Isa. 32:17).

When discouraged: "Be strong and take heart, all you who hope in the LORD" (Ps. 31:24).

For deliverance from distress and trouble: "Then they cried to the LORD in their trouble, and he saved them from their distress" (Ps. 107:13).

Now, some thirty years later, in another town and another church setting, I am grateful for my current pastor and for the radio teachers I listen to. Between them all, I am learning topically, contextually, and exegetically. And I know there is still so much more knowledge to acquire.

What Are You Going to Do?

You can continue to carry around words from your past—or from just the other day—that demean, reject, and discourage you. If you have words like these ringing in your ears, you have a choice. Will you continue to believe them and let them rule your life, or will you choose to see them for what they are and, through prayer, replace those words with what God says about you?

What's important to know is obtaining freedom is a process. While the God of all creation, in the twinkling of an eye, can free us instantly and completely from every bondage, in His grace and mercy, He often allows us to "go through" and "rise above." Many of us carry around so many hurts that we might need to experience gradual change, not only for our benefit but also for the benefit of those in our immediate realm of influence.

Change is possible, and complete release is available.

So Then, What Is Prayer?

Simply put, prayer is talking with God. It is having a conversation with your Creator—the One who knows you better than you know yourself, the One who has your best interest in mind, the One who knows the beginning from the end because He is the Alpha and the Omega (Rev. 22:13), the One who knows what you need and will supply it accordingly (Phil. 4:19), the only One who will love you unconditionally and with no reserve.

Prayer replaces what the world, your mind, your parents, and the enemy have to say about you with the Word of God. Instead of fear, operate in faith. Instead of anger, operate in grace. Instead of doubt, operate in belief.

Once again, we have taken a huge topic, prayer, and tried to wrap it up in a few pages. What is key is the importance of using prayer to break the power of negative and hurtful words spoken to or about you.

To *break* means to crush something into small pieces. Think of prayer as a sledgehammer. Demolish whatever it is that causes you anxiety with the sledgehammer of prayer, breaking up those concrete monuments and memorials. What now is in tiny fragments can only become a stronghold again if you make the choice to gather up the pieces and put them back together. It's time to take personal responsibility for your own well-being; don't give that power over to someone else. Read on and be blessed. Your freedom might be just around the next corner.

it's **your** turn

1. After reading this chapter, how do you feel about how casually a curse can be spoken into someone's life? How does this realization encourage you to be more careful when you speak?

2. Are there words still haunting you today? If so, list them here and then go to God's Word and write out what He says about you. Finally, pray these words over yourself.

3. How do you feel about the adage "Act the way you want to become, and you'll become the way you act"? In what areas could you apply this to your life?

4. From the thoughts presented in this chapter, in what ways have you been encouraged to pray?

6

walking in freedom

Just living is not enough. . . . One must have sunshine, freedom, and a little flower.

HANS CHRISTIAN ANDERSEN

Thus far on our journey together, we've looked at words that may have had long-term effects on our lives, both positive and negative. We've come to recognize that most of the negativity thrown our way was not about us but rather about the person speaking. We've chosen to take steps to extend forgiveness where necessary to free ourselves. We've gone into the Bible and replaced harmful remarks with what God, our Creator, says about us. And through prayer, we've learned how to break any remaining power someone's words have over us.

Does that mean we are totally free? More than likely, there's still work for many of us to do. But if we believe change can happen and we are taking steps in the right direction, God will meet us each step of the way and help us reach a level of healing and freedom. And He will not only meet us at each step, no matter how large or small that step might be, but also urge us forward on our personal journeys of finding wholeness and freedom from hurtful words.

How do we walk in this newfound freedom God has for each of us, even when our freedom is not yet complete? I will offer six vital steps to take, but first we must understand what an offense is and why we are so easily offended.

The dictionary defines the word *offense* as "a breach of a law or rule, an illegal act, an annoyance or resentment brought about by a perceived insult to or disregard for one-self or one's standards or principles." For our purposes, we'll look at the second part of this definition: *an annoyance or resentment brought about by a perceived insult to or disregard for oneself or one's standards or principles.* Although not part of the definition, we know by experience that once offended we can become annoyed to the point of exasperation, anger, bitterness, and much more.

I'll use a couple examples from my own life to show what this might look like. If I haven't already mentioned it, I will go on record now as saying I love chocolate, good chocolate, rich chocolate, like Godiva chocolate. Over the years, I've been blessed with extraordinary gifts of chocolate. In fact, I have some interesting stories related to how and from where these gifts emerged.

At times, I've had an overabundance of chocolate, and my husband has suggested I give some of it away. In the same vein, if I've received a gift similar to something I already have, such as a kitchen gadget (something I love to collect), he has suggested I pass it on. It's important to note that Bob is a minimalist to the nth degree. He is not in the least attached to things. He says it comes from not having a lot growing up and from his army days when he was in a STRAC (Strategic Army Corp) division. That's when you are Standing Tall Right Around the Clock, equipped and ready to go anyplace in the world at a moment's notice, which means you will not be taking much with you. Not a bad way to live, really.

I love to gift others as much as Bob. But when I gift someone, I want it to be my idea, not Bob's. I remember thinking, *If you want to give your things away, go ahead. If I want to give my things away, that will be my choice to make.* Yes, I've had this mental conversation, I'm embarrassed to say. What's more important, however, was finding out why Bob's suggestions bothered me. In fact, more than bothering me, his suggestions even offended me.

Not desiring to be selfish about "my things," I asked the Lord to show me why Bob's recommendations brought me such angst. Immediately, I was reminded of my elementary school days. It was my responsibility to clean my room, but occasionally Mom would do it for me. When she did, she often threw things away without asking if I wanted or needed them.

I didn't realize it then, but as I matured, I began to feel that when someone throws or gives away something of yours without checking with you first, the implication is that what you value and see as important doesn't matter. And it's taking away a choice that's clearly yours to make. Mom was merely doing me a favor by cleaning my room. But without realizing it, I misinterpreted her actions to mean I wasn't worthy. In some way, I was violated, but I didn't understand it then.

Likewise, Bob was not intending to break my spirit or deem me unworthy when he suggested I give something of mine away. He was merely operating in his conservative, seeing-a-need-and-filling-it way of doing things. There was nothing wrong in that.

When I explained to him that I'd like to make the choice about what I give and when and how I felt about Mom making those choices for me so many years ago, he respectfully understood.

Although not having to do with words, here's another example of a perceived offense. There was a time in my married life when I could not understand why I was offended when Bob passed behind me and took a swipe at my bottom, a perfectly fine and normal thing for a husband to do. Except when he did, I felt annoyed and insulted. *But why?* I wondered. I even mentioned it to him, saying that when he touched me like that, I felt uncomfortable, even offended.

Again, I asked the Lord for insight. "Why, Father, would something so natural make me feel uncomfortable, almost violated?" As before, this time the Lord showed me a picture from my preteen years when I went with neighbors to a Michigan lake to picnic and enjoy the water. Several neighbor boys went along. In fact, of the seven children, five were boys. Is it any surprise they loved dunking each other and us girls?

One of them, however, would come up underwater from behind and grab me, leaving me feeling helpless, embarrassed, and extremely uncomfortable. As soon as the Lord brought that picture to my remembrance, I gasped. There it was. Now every time my husband passed behind me and gently took a swipe, I felt violated, insulted, and helpless. Once I came to this realization, I was able to replace those feelings of humiliation with natural emotions. Amazingly, God used a perceived offense to help bring me healing, personally and in my marriage.

By my examples, can you see that what one person might see as something normal another could see as offensive? By delving just under the surface, old memories can be brought to light and dealt with, which, in turn, can bring healing and freedom.

Offenses Will Happen

Be assured, offenses will come about. We've already given reasons why. But now that we've come to some basic understandings of human nature, about the brokenness of others, and of *why* we become offended, we can take steps to guard against how offenses impact us.

Step 1: Expect to Be Offended

Offenses will occur. Like the two I mentioned, there may be deep-seated reasons for what we see as violations. We might be tired or hungry, or maybe we only heard part of what was said. In both of my experiences, when dealt with, they brought much-needed healing. And please don't forget, the words you might consider offensive may just be the result of someone else's weariness all the way to a broken heart.

Step 2: Stand Your Ground

Is this about being belligerent or obstinate or needing to have your own way? Not at all. It's about remaining steadfast in what you've accomplished thus far on your journey toward freedom. It's about keeping the proper perspective when it comes to the words—and actions—of others toward you. It's about looking at them through the eyes of understanding and compassion. It's about making a deliberate effort to extend forgiveness and grace, even when you'd rather not. And it's about keeping in mind what your Creator says about you.

How best to stand your ground? It's most effective if you write out what ground you are going to occupy and protect. Begin by making a list of what you've discovered from the chapters thus far. Write out names, what was said, and what you've chosen to forgive. Write out what the Lord says about you in His Word. Keep these lists handy so you can remind yourself of the ground you have achieved and will maintain. No one can take from you what you've attained thus far. Remember, you are in the driver's seat. You are no longer under but rather *above* the circumstances—or words. Do not relinquish this position to anyone else.

If you have some doors you need to totally close, now might be a good time to make note of them. Then, at your earliest convenience, start banging those doors shut and locking them with the key you hold in your hand: your key of empowerment.

Another door you might need to use your key on is that of being a victim. When you released that certain someone from the words they spoke to you that tended to lock you away in your prison of words, you made a declaration that you are no longer a victim. There will be no more "poor me" and "but life isn't fair" statements. You will no longer be stuck in your past; instead, you are taking positive steps into your future.

Another way to stand your ground or maintain the freedom you have worked so hard to attain is to keep your roots deeply planted in the things of the Lord. Spend time regularly with Him in His Word and in prayer, gather with other believers for fellowship and accountability, and regularly sing songs of praise to the wonderful God He is.

Here's how I stand my ground. Daily, I endeavor to get into the Word of God, either by reading and meditating on portions of Scripture or by listening to teachers and preachers; I sing along with worshipful music that honors and glorifies my King; I seek God's guidance for each day; and I associate with other believers on a regular basis. It's not hard to do. If I can do it, so can you.

Yes, I check social media. Yes, from time to time, news surfaces on my computer screen and I expose myself to what's going on in the world around me. But my goal is to balance all that by staying rooted in the Lord. In fact, I make it a point to tip the scales in that direction. I'm careful about what goes through the gates of my eyes and ears, the doorways into my soul. I implore you to do the same.

Step 3: Have Realistic Expectations

So often we are disappointed in others because they did not meet our expectations, whether in what they said or what they did. They didn't say the exact words we were looking for, and therefore they missed the mark. And now we are tempted to hold that against them, thinking they really don't care. It's not wrong to have high expectations, but those high expectations should be placed on ourselves and not on others.

Other people will disappoint. They will make promises they're not able to keep. They will say one thing and do another. We wish it weren't so, but we humans are fallible. We are broken, and we come with no guarantees. Maybe that's why Scripture tells us:

> It is better to take refuge in the LORD
>   than to trust in humans. (Ps. 118:8)

I don't advocate you should expect the worst in others and then appreciate when they do come through. That kind of attitude is negative at best. Rather, place realistic expectations on people and show your appreciation when they exceed what you had hoped for.

Give others the benefit of the doubt. We can be hasty to cast a bad light on someone's words or actions, especially if we've taken the words or deeds out of context or if we don't know the whole story. We see it on social media daily—half-truths, misleading headlines, varying opinions. Unfortunately, we are inclined to believe the negative.

In an article titled "Our Brain's Negative Bias," writer Hara Estroff Marano reports that according to studies done by John Cacioppo, PhD, University of Chicago, the brain reacts more strongly to stimuli it deems negative. Cacioppo found that there is a greater surge in electrical activity when viewing negative images versus positive images. In other words, our brains are negatively biased. Further, because of the disproportionate weight of the negative on our brains, a healthy balance does not equate to a 50-50 equilibrium. Rather, studies show the magic ratio to be five to one.[1]

What does that say about words spoken to us and words we speak to others? That's right, it takes at least five positive comments to balance out the one negative comment we either hear or deliver.

What about "if-only" thinking? That's when we blame anyone and anything but ourselves for our disappointments in life: *if only* he hadn't treated me that way, *if only* I were taller (or shorter), *if only* I could live in a warmer climate. If-only thinking takes away from what we have and causes us to focus on what we don't have, like a missing ceiling tile or two. Exchange if-only thinking with an attitude of gratitude. You'll be happier in the long run, and those with whom you live and work will benefit as well from your more positive attitude.

Step 4: Set Healthy Boundaries

Setting boundaries does not mean having to wear a shield of protection at all times or developing a hard heart. And it's not about analyzing everything that's said and done. Interestingly, boundary setting is another topic with a vast amount of resources available. How about a staggering nearly 49,000 books with the word *boundaries* somewhere in their titles. That's amazing and suggests we humans need to know what healthy boundaries are and how to use them wisely.

Earlier we discussed that to forgive someone for the hurtful and damaging words that have been spoken does not mean we are obliged to allow them to continue their disrespectful treatment, no matter the whys for their actions. When that's the case, there are those we may need to eliminate from our social circle. Some we might need to associate with only occasionally. But what about the ones we see every day in our homes or our places of employment? What then?

Sometimes boundaries are not physical, especially with those we need to deal with daily who spew unhealthy and damaging words our way. In those cases, we need to set up internal boundaries.

We all have them in our lives—the "Donny Downers" or "Negative Nellies"—people who, often unconsciously, bring you down with their negative comments. They tend to rain on your parade, so to speak, not happy for you in your accomplishments or dreams. They often see every glass half empty instead of half full. And they downplay the lives of others when all you want is to have a pleasant conversation.

If possible, limit the amount of time you spend with people who bring you down. Sometimes it's necessary to end a relationship if it's that toxic, which is usually not an easy thing to do, especially for someone like myself who prefers to keep relationships tidy and who will, at all costs, work to keep the peace. I saw too much turmoil growing up. My stomach still churns when I hear people raise their voices at one another.

When I've been in uncomfortable situations and have needed to call a halt to an association, I have resorted to prayer, something like, "Heavenly Father, resolve this relationship and create it to be what You'd like it to be, or bring it to an end." I'm often amazed at how orderly He works things out. In most cases, I have not had to say or do a thing, and somehow or another, the situation worked itself out.

Step 5: Seek Accountability

For many, addictions become a way of life as we try to drown out the words from our pasts, words that say we are worthless and that we'll never amount to anything, words that compare us with others, words that degrade and demean us, words the enemy will use to accuse and abuse us.

Words aren't the only things that drive us to our vices. Perhaps it's physical abuse, poor living conditions, or a myriad of other negative experiences, whether we are younger or older. And so we try to escape to a happier place, at least a place where we can forget for a while. To get some relief, we turn to food, drugs, alcohol, and more. It's all too common. But too soon, what we tried for a time wasn't enough, and so the use became amplified. In some cases, addictions have consumed us, and we need outside help in addition to personal accountability.

Two proven groups I am most familiar with for help with addictions are Celebrate Recovery and Teen Challenge. Celebrate Recovery is nonresidential with weekly meetings. A Christ-centered recovery program, it began twenty-six years ago and is now in 30,000 churches worldwide. Teen Challenge, with a history of sixty years, is also Christ-centered with both residential and nonresidential recovery programs for teens and adults. Sometimes we just need a little more accountability. These groups and others like them are equipped to offer what most of our families and friends cannot.

Step 6: Forgive Daily

Do you recall in chapter 3 we explored what it means to forgive others the way God in Christ forgave us? Again, how

109

did He forgive us? First, He forgave us once and for all. Next, He forgives us daily as we lay our faults before Him and in true repentance ask for His forgiveness. Finally, He forgave us long before we ever sinned. In fact, He forgave us before we were even born.

How does this relate to our walking in freedom? It's the way we need to forgive others: once and for all, over and over again, and before they even offend us. That's one big order, but if we can master forgiving others, then we will be better equipped to walk in freedom. Soon, words others say will bounce off us. We will immediately perceive that the words emanated from some hurt or malfunction in the lives of the ones who issued them. And we will extend grace even before it's required.

How Will You Know?

When you have truly forgiven someone, one or many of the following indicators will be evident:

1. When you think of the person who offended you, you no longer feel negatively toward them. You may even feel a love you never felt before, a love that looks beyond their faults and sees their needs, just like the love God has for you and me.
2. You won't feel the need to change the other person. Truly, that's up to them and God. We can only work to change ourselves, and even that is with help from the Lord.
3. You will be more concerned about the person than you will about how they offended you, especially

as you become acquainted with their story. The offenses you once felt will tend to fade into the background. In fact, there may come a time when you wonder why you felt offended in the first place.

4. You may find ways to enjoy being around the other person. Depending upon their relationship to you, especially if they are a family member and it is necessary from time to time to be around them, you will look for what you have in common and bond accordingly.

5. You will no longer feel it necessary to blame the other person for your own actions and words. A maturity follows forgiving someone. Once we extend forgiveness, we begin to take responsibility for our actions, realizing that even when we felt inclined to act inappropriately because of someone else's harmful words, we made a choice to act that way.

6. You will feel empowered when around the other person or when thinking about them. You will no longer feel like you're an object to be used or abused by them.

These are just a few of the ways you might feel when you've truly extended the kind of forgiveness God extends to us. You might have additional ways to add to this list. Please do so at the end of this chapter. Make this a journal of sorts to show the steps you've taken to move on in your freedom from hurting words.

What True Freedom Looks Like

Imagine yourself enjoying lunch with your mother, who, let's say for the sake of this example, tends to rain on your parade, offers advice when you haven't asked, and/or compares you with your siblings. This time, be ready up front to forgive. Prepare your heart to be grateful for the time to spend with your parent. Instead of dreading the encounter, seat yourself prayed up and in an attitude of gratitude and empowerment because you have forgiven her for her past sins against you. Before she even says a word, forgive her. Throughout your conversation, offer grace and mercy and compassion as you pray that somehow and in some way God will grab hold of her heart and heal the broken places, just as He is healing yours.

Remember, words will be spoken to us daily. How we respond or react to those words is up to us and absolutely no one else. Make a choice today to walk in true freedom from hurting words.

it's **your** turn

1. I gave two examples of perceived offenses and then showed how I was able to move beyond their effects. List examples of perceived offenses in your life and what you can do to move forward.

2. Of the six steps offered to walk in freedom from hurting words, which spoke the loudest to you?

3. Keeping in mind that it takes at least five positive statements to offset one negative statement, what can you do today to ensure that your words said to others (and to yourself) provide a healthy balance in the lives of those important to you?

4. Closing out the chapter are six indicators that you've truly forgiven someone. Which of these have you already experienced?

PART 2

words we speak to ourselves

Words are the most powerful thing in the universe. Words are containers. They contain faith, or fear, and they produce after their kind. Your words are building blocks of which you construct your life and future.

CHARLES CAPPS

7

self-talk—we all do it

If someone else's words tear you down, use your own words
to build yourself up!

I n her book *Seated with Christ,* Dr. Heather Holleman
writes that her college roommate said to her one day,
"You spend more time than anyone I know looking at
your nose in the mirror." About her nose, Heather says, "The
wound is deep."

In ninth grade, the "most gorgeous boy in school," according to Heather, turned around in his seat in front of her
on the school bus to say hello. And then he asked, "Why do
you have all of those little black dots on your nose? What
are those?" Obviously, there was no place for her to run
and hide.

"What was I supposed to say? Let me introduce you to my enormous pores? They are pores. They are blackheads. They are the worst feature on my substantial nose." Instead, she said to Mr. Gorgeous, mortified, "I don't know."

He leaned in closer and asked, "Do I have them on my nose?" Well, no, he didn't. She said his nose was perfect.[1]

Heather cried in her bedroom that night, and even more, she agonized every morning as she looked into her mirror, squeezing, covering in thick foundation, and powdering in an attempt to send her nose "into hiding."

And so she thought about herself all day long but not in a positive way. Her appearance dominated her thoughts, and she carried those thoughts into adulthood. When she became tired of all her insecurity, she began to search the Scriptures and found that when King David, for example, felt the most insecure, he concentrated on something other than himself. David chose to fix his eyes on the beauty of the Lord instead (Ps. 27:4).

Heather was blessed to come to the realization that people who are seated with Christ don't have to worry about their appearance. Rather, when they come to a true understanding of who they are in Christ and that they are seated in heavenly places with Him, they can take their eyes off themselves because they are too busy adoring the beauty of the Creator.

But what of those who have not yet come to that understanding? There are a lot of "Heathers" out there, looking daily into the mirror and disliking what they see. They may even despise what they see—and they think nothing of letting themselves know. It's called *self-talk*, and it's something we all do whether we like the reflection we see or not.

What Is Self-Talk?

Self-talk is defined as the act or practice of talking to one-self, either aloud or silently and mentally. I do both. I have since my early childhood, and I do today. I remember getting caught in my world of make-believe a ton of years ago under my grandmother's dining room table. I was admonished for talking to myself and to my dolls, with the inference that those who talk to themselves are mentally ill. I'm glad my little-girl world overruled that implication, although I do re-call feeling a little stifled after that when visiting Grandma and Grandpa.

Talking to ourselves being a sign of mental illness is an old wives' tale, for sure, since research today shows that talking to oneself is perfectly normal and, in fact, is deemed healthy. Linda Sapadin, PhD, writes about it on her website in a post titled "Talking to Yourself—a Sign of Sanity."[2]

It's healthy—that is, if you are speaking positively to your-self. We can surmise that when young Heather looked in the mirror, she was not reciting positive comments about her appearance. Of course, she learned later to focus her vision on the beauty of Christ. Before that, however, she concen-trated on a facial feature she was not happy with, and she did it often, according to her college roommate.

What Do I See When I Look at Me?

I think there are more "Heathers" than not, so I want to focus the next few pages on what we tend to see when we look in our own mirrors, either literally or theoretically. I'm of-fering five areas or categories we see when we look at our reflections: physical appearance, intellect, capabilities, position in life, and family line. Let's explore them one by one.

Physical Appearance

The most probable aspect we see when we gaze into a mirror is our physical features, which include every facet of what we look like. I don't know about you, but I don't tend to look in the mirror and see my positive features, even though positive features are something we all have. No, I tend to focus on what's wrong with what I see.

Currently, I see graying hair, sagging skin, more weight than I'd like to carry, and the list goes on. Heather focused on her nose. I'm inclined to focus on the fact that I'm looking older with each passing twenty-four hours. And if I'm not careful, I can get into a funk, which then affects the rest of my day. I know I'm not alone.

Another thing I see when I look in the mirror is features I don't have but would like to have. Remember, we talked about the Missing Tile Syndrome in part 1. That's when we walk into a crowded room and almost immediately see features on others we'd like to have but don't. Or we see glimpses of those "tiles" on our social media friends. Worse, we might see them on personalities and celebrities whose photos likely have been digitally edited and glamourized. Can you relate?

Intellect

Now an adult in her sixties, Jennifer recalls many words spoken to her by her four brothers. Being smack dab in the middle age-wise and the only girl, she was subjected to a lot of teasing by all those boys. Often, their words were harsh. Sometimes they were spoken in the presence of her brothers' friends.

Adding to the angst of what Jennifer felt from her brothers' hurtful words was the fact that while nearly all the boys were all-A students, Jennifer's grades were only average.

Jennifer knows her mother meant well, but her words when trying to console her daughter went something like this: "Jennifer, you'll just be getting married and having babies when you grow up." Her mom's implication was to leave the good grades to the boys, which left Jennifer believing that, indeed, she was not intelligent and it really didn't matter.

No one told this young girl that she, in fact, was filled with tremendous potential for intellect and so much more. Only recently has Jennifer been able to see these words for what they were and how they affected her self-talk for many years.

Capabilities

Sonya Copeland's highest grade in school was third grade.[3] When she was thirteen, she married a man fifteen years her senior. It is said that Robert Carson rescued young Sonya from a home life of poverty and abuse.

At twenty years of age, Sonya had her first son, Curtis. Two years later, she had her second son, Benjamin. When the boys were ten and eight, Sonya and her husband separated. Surely, when this young woman looked in the mirror, she could wonder about her capabilities. What could a woman with a third-grade education, coming from poverty and abuse and subsequently divorce, have to offer?

What Sonya Copeland Carson did have was a determination to see her sons accomplish what she could not. Putting everything she had into her boys, Sonya took measures to ensure her sons would be successful. And her hard work paid off.

Today, we know one of her sons, Dr. Ben Carson, as the seventeenth United States Secretary of Housing and Urban Development. His illustrious career includes graduating from Yale University and University of Michigan Medical School. He performed groundbreaking surgery to successfully separate conjoined twins, and he became the youngest chief of pediatric neurosurgery at the age of thirty-three. His list of accomplishments is long, and he credits it all to the driving force of his mother, who was much more capable than she ever could imagine.

Position in Life

While growing up, I dreamed of being a teacher. I loved school and poured my life into my classes, friendships, and activities. Often, I set up a classroom in my bedroom where my little sister and her best friend acted as my pupils.

An all-A student for most of my school years, I received a scholarship upon graduation to attend our local community college. But before finishing the first semester and shortly after my nineteenth birthday, I exchanged my dreams of college and a teaching career for a wedding dress and homemaking responsibilities. Fifteen months later, I became a mama for the first time, and by the time I was twenty-five, I had my three children.

High school classmates who had gone off to college to pursue their dreams—and mine—called from time to time to share about college life, while I, on the other hand, stayed home to raise my little ones and learn to bake pies (which I still love to do). Looking back, I am grateful to have been able to have my children when I was so young and still have plenty of years left for career building. Back then, however, when I looked in the mirror, I saw a bedraggled-looking young woman whose station in life was far from what she had always imagined. As you can guess, my self-talk was not positive at those times.

Family Line

Evan Andrews wrote a piece in 2013 titled "7 Amazing Rags to Riches Stories"[4] in which he features the lives of several individuals whose family lines were nothing to boast about.

For example, Evan writes of Russian Empress Catherine I, who was born in 1684 into a family of Lithuanian peasants and later orphaned at the age of three. Steel magnate Andrew Carnegie, born in 1835, began life in a family of destitute laborers. Biddy Mason, born a slave, later found fortune as one of America's first female real estate tycoons. Charles Dickens navigated his way through a hardscrabble childhood in England in the 1820s to become one of the nineteenth century's literary masters.

In addition, we know of Agnes Gonxha Boyaxiu, born in Macedonia in 1910 of Albanian grocers. Agnes became Mother Teresa of Calcutta, ministering for most of her life to the poorest of the poor. She was eventually awarded the Nobel Peace Prize.

Biblically, King David began his career as a shepherd boy.

When I gaze into the mirror today, I see a little Assyrian girl from Flint, Michigan, born into dysfunction and meagerness. While I do not count myself in the ranks of Empress Catherine, Andrew Carnegie, Biddy Mason, Charles Dickens, Mother Teresa, or King David, what we all have in common is our Creator God. Made in His likeness, we are fully equipped with the potential to accomplish His plans and purposes, and that against all human odds and the world's common recipes for success. You have the same Creator and master planner. What do you see when you look at your reflection in the mirror?

Oh, what a tangled web we weave when first we practice the game of comparison. Do you see in each of the categories above how, instead of accepting who we are, we compare ourselves to others "more beautiful or handsome," "more intellectual," "more accomplished," "in more enviable positions," "as having a better heritage"? Instead of appreciating what God has given us in these areas, we become covetous, ungrateful, negative, complaining, and quite frankly not the kind of people others want to be around.

How Words Affect What We See in the Mirror

How do words spoken to us early in our lives, or maybe just yesterday, have anything to do with what we see in the mirror? Too often, what we see in our reflection is based on another's words, those of a parent or other family member, a teacher, a coach, someone in the clergy, a friend, a spouse—you name it. Even in the case of Dr. Holleman, had not the most gorgeous boy in the world pointed out the blemishes on her nose (something natural for an adolescent to have), perhaps her nose might never have become an issue for her, a burden she carried that affected her life for years.

What are some of the words you've heard? When you look in the mirror, do those words, whether positive or negative, ever poke through from the recesses of your mind? And do you repeat them to yourself?

For example, in the area of our physical selves, has anyone ever told you that you are too tall, too short, too skinny, too fat, maybe homely?

How about intellect? Were the words "You're stupid" ever spoken to you?

Regarding capability, has anyone ever said, "You can't do anything right"?

How about your family background? Did you ever hear words such as "You're a loser, just like your Uncle Joe"?

And now when you look in the mirror, do you repeat those words to yourself, aloud or silently? That's negative self-talk. And here's the unsuspected danger in all that. Are you ready for this? What you perceive and speak about yourself, you tend to become. That's right. Your own words can help create and perpetuate something about yourself you don't like. Some call it a self-fulfilling prophecy, which is defined as a prediction that directly or indirectly causes itself to become true. Why? Because what you believe affects your behavior.

Think about it. If I believe I'm not attractive or intelligent or capable, I will probably act accordingly. I might stand back like a wallflower, never trying anything new or presenting my opinion. If I feel that my position in life or my family heritage is less than that of others, I will most likely act as though I am of little value and have nothing to offer. We've all heard the admonition in the diet industry: we are what we eat. In this case, we are what our words say we are.

In direct sales, we're taught that what we think about, we talk about; and what we talk about, we bring about. I believe this is true in every area of our lives. If I think I'm ugly, I speak accordingly to myself and possibly to others. And the more I talk about being ugly, the more I begin to act the words out, thereby sealing my own fate of what I don't want to be. Can you see how this works? Is there evidence that you're defining who you are with your words?

It Doesn't Have to Be That Way

You can live a fulfilled and joy-filled life. It all depends on your attitude and the choices you make, two areas you alone are responsible for. Others may try to influence you with their words either to or about you, but ultimately you are the one in control.

Keep in mind what you've discovered from previous chapters. Most if not all the negative words spoken to or about you *are not about you*. And you've chosen to move on in life through forgiveness—what you received from God and what you have extended to others. Now live like it! And how do you do that? I'm glad you asked.

First, *stop* speaking negatively about yourself. Second, *stop* dragging others down with you. "It's not easy just to stop," you say? Let's consider a few things.

Nothing Positive Comes from Negativity

When we focus on the negative self-talk we're all occasionally guilty of instead of on the positive aspects of ourselves, our negativity tends to leak out onto others. You see, when we don't care for or like something about ourselves, our negative self-talk can turn into grumbling and complaining, which besides being displeasing to God is harmful in the practical sense.

Realistically, everyone is going to complain from time to time. I'd like to believe 100 percent of the time I'm positive, saying good things about everything and everyone. Unfortunately, that just isn't so. What I'm talking about here is a negative attitude that becomes more natural than not for a person.

According to Dr. Robin Kowalski, professor of psychology at Clemson University, there are three common types of complainers.[5]

There are the *venters*. These people want to be heard, seeking others to listen to their complaints. Even when good advice is given, they are often quick to shut down solutions.

There are *sympathy seekers*. They always have it worse than you and are quick to see faults in others. In addition, they prefer to be victims.

There are *chronic complainers*, who tend to ruminate or think obsessively about something. Then they complain about it to others. Their complaining doesn't bring them relief, however. No, they become worried and anxious about something that is usually out of their control—and often none of their business. And they just can't seem to let some things go.

Dr. Kowalski further explains that this kind of negativity can rewire the brains of those who complain and send them into a downward spiral, meaning the more they focus on the problem instead of the solution, the more they eventually learn to see the negative in everything.

There's nothing wrong with venting at the proper time and in the proper place and in a reasonable way, but it's important that we quickly move on to a resolution. It's important to protect ourselves from that downward spiral that leads to absolutely nothing positive.

What Song Are You Singing?

Additional research shows that repeated complaining rewires our brains to make future complaining more likely.[6] Over time, a person will find it's easier to be negative than to be positive, regardless of what's happening around them. Complaining becomes their default behavior. And now others perceive that person as a grumbler.

What words emanate from your mouth to others or to yourself? What words do you tap out in emails or post on social media? In other words, what "song" are you singing when you are communicating with family, friends, and coworkers? Are you coming across as a "poor-me victim," "Negative Nellie," "fault finder," "blame placer," and a myriad of other negative labels? Beware that your words will not only create your situation but will also define you.

The Mind-Body Connection

When we are being negative, our bodies release the stress hormone *cortisol*, which shifts us into the fight-or-flight mode. That, in turn, raises our blood pressure and blood sugar so we'll be prepared to escape if need be or to defend ourselves. All the extra cortisol that's been released from complaining then impairs our immune systems, thereby making us more susceptible to high cholesterol, diabetes, heart disease, and obesity. It even makes the brain more vulnerable to strokes. This set of facts alone ought to provide sufficient, compelling reason for any complainer to "stop it!"

Neuronal Mirroring

Our negativity not only brings us down but also has a stark effect on those around us. Another study shows that since we human beings are inherently social, we tend to naturally or subconsciously mimic the moods of those around us, particularly people with whom we spend a lot of time. This process is called *neuronal mirroring*. It is the basis of our ability to feel empathy.

If we don't want our negative thinking and complaining to affect others, we need to make vital changes. And if we don't want to become a complainer, we need to be careful about whom we hang out with on a regular basis. If we find ourselves in situations in which we regularly come in contact with negative people, we may need to set some personal boundaries.

Someone Else's Fault

When we look in the mirror, make our comparisons, talk negatively to ourselves, and then conclude we don't measure up, we tend to play the blame game.

This game isn't in a box with game pieces and a board. This is when we blame everyone and everything for what ails us, including our current state of affairs. We blame our parents, siblings, spouses, friends, neighbors, coworkers, supervisors, or elected officials. And the list goes on. In blaming others for the way we are or for the situations in which we find ourselves, we might say:

> If it weren't for my husband dragging me across the country because of his job, I wouldn't be in this mess.
>
> If it weren't for my parents, who were drunk most of the time, I wouldn't have to attend these meetings.
>
> If it weren't for my older brother who excelled in school, I wouldn't have to be the brunt of criticism from his former teachers who expect me to be more like him.

And you know, there is some validity to these assessments. Sometimes we're in situations not of our own making. Sometimes we're at the mercy of others. Sometimes we're limited in what we can do by the actions of another person. But playing the blame game does nothing but add to our frustration and negative self-talk.

Regrets, I've Had a Few

Sometimes our circumstances are the result of our own doing. Sometimes when we look in the mirror, we see a person who made choices that weren't the best. Sometimes we see someone who'd give their eye teeth to live life all over again—with the knowledge and wisdom we now have. I can relate to that sort of wishing, for sure.

What we have here is something called *regret*. That's when we feel sad, repentant, or disappointed over something that has happened or been done, especially in regard to a loss or missed opportunity. Did I already say I can relate?

Oh, how I'd love to live some of my years over. There are many things I'd do differently in the areas of relationships, parenting, and many others. But since that's not possible, I choose to take steps that keep me moving forward, unencumbered by lost youth, poor decision-making, and negative self-talk. How will you stop speaking negatively about yourself and dragging others down with you? Perhaps you'd like to take some of the following steps as well.

Develop an Attitude of Gratitude

Almost consistently in my research, when it comes to getting out of ourselves and going from a propensity for negativity to a more positive mindset, developing an attitude of gratitude surfaced time and again. There are numerous resources for learning how to be more grateful, so I'm not going to elaborate. But I can testify, thankfulness works every time. Life takes on much more meaning when I practice gratitude for who I am and what I have instead of remorse for who I am not and what I do not possess. It will work for you too.

Look for the Good

Even in the direst of circumstances, you can find something good. Here in Florida, we just experienced a Category 5 hurricane. You may remember her name: Irma. By the time it got to our immediate area, it was a Category 3, but it still left a wake of damage and power outages throughout our county.

As Irma began to make her way west from the Caribbean, Bob and I received an invitation to travel north to seek safety with family members in Georgia. We determined early on, however, that with four older, single women in our immediate neighborhood and with our youngest son and his family also in town, we were not going to evacuate to a place of safety without them. So we stayed and are glad we did.

Two of the women in our cul-de-sac had friends or family nearby. The other two were alone throughout the entire experience. We checked on them several times before Irma blew through Central Florida to make sure they were prepared, and we looked in on them afterward to see how they fared. Prior to the storm, we knew these ladies from neighborhood get-togethers, but now we know them more personally and our lives are far richer.

One bonus is that one of the women owns Molly, an eight-year-old Shih Tzu. Because of health issues, my neighbor can no longer take Molly for walks. A short time before the storm, I had prayed the Lord would bring a dog into our lives, a good reason to regularly get up from my sedentary editorial life and walk. Thanks to Hurricane Irma, I now have a walking partner. I'm more fit, Molly is a happy little canine camper, and my neighbor is grateful.

Yes, hurricanes are destructive and nasty, but if you look hard enough you can find something positive, even in a whirlwind.

Change Your Thinking and Learn to Shift Gears

Out of the blue, words were spoken that shut me down. It doesn't matter who spoke the words. The point is, even though I knew them to be emanating from old wounds, in my vulnerability, I took them as a personal affront. Immediately, my mind started playing old games.

Why, Lord? I mentally mumbled. *I don't need this. I'm weary*... and my song took form. Soon, similar times flooded from the recesses of my mind. One affront was added to another, and I could feel myself turning inward, my self-talk becoming more negative. If anything, I reverted to thinking like a victim.

I felt pressure in my head, probably from holding back tears I should have let fall. I became steely in my countenance and heart. Darkness threatened to overtake me—and then I remembered I had a choice. I could continue in the downward spiral, or I could choose to focus on something more positive. I could go further inward, or I could look beyond myself. I could wallow, or I could get up from the mire that was pulling me under. Thankfully, I chose to make a call to check on my neighbor and set up my next walking date with Molly.

I know words will come—words that offend, hurt, perhaps even demean—but I have a choice and so do you. When words come at me that threaten my well-being, will I wallow or (in my case) will I walk? Will I ruminate or will I remember my blessings and my own shortcomings? Will I warm up my vocal cords to sing the "somebody done me wrong" song or will I sing praises to the King of Kings and Lord of Lords who always has my best interest in mind? Will I revert to my old victim mentality or will I step out into the world where the sky is the limit and where with Christ I can do all things?

You may be faced with these same kinds of choices. What will you choose?

Once I made up my mind that day to stop the negativity and let it go, I touched up my makeup, fixed a cup of coffee, and then sat down to write this fresh and new example of what can happen when we least expect it.

Create an Environment for Success

I follow several proponents of whole food, plant-based eating. Many suggest that to be effective in this style of eating—or in any endeavor, for that matter—we need to create environments for success. Because they know that certain restricted foods can be temptations, and one bite can lead to two, they don't even bring those foods into their homes. Thus, they have created environments for success.

Likewise, when I consider creating for myself an environment for success when it comes to self-talk, what elements do I need to eliminate or not let into my surroundings? Certain books, TV programs, social media sites, music? If I want to live successfully and eliminate negative self-talk, then I need to make wise choices about what I allow to influence me. And I just may have to clean house—in more ways than one.

In her book *On a Tightrope: Experiences with God*, Sharyn Albright writes about a relationship she was admonished by the Lord to sever, and she thought she had closed all the necessary doors. What she hadn't done, however, was to throw away letters—beautifully decorated works of art—she had received from her friend. Sharyn knew she shouldn't keep those letters, but she couldn't bear to destroy them. They were only letters, after all, so she hid them away in a metal cabinet.

"Somehow I thought encasing the letters and getting them out of my sight would protect me from their influence. Not so. The problem is I knew they were in the cabinet." Sharyn understood that the enemy of her soul was using those letters to lure and influence her and to continue to hold her in bondage. She knew what had to be done. She got up out of bed one night and gathered up scissors, the letters, and a trash bag.

"I continued to blubber as I read each one and cut them into little pieces. Later that morning, I emptied the bag into the barbeque pit and burned everything."[7] She had now finally closed all the necessary doors, which resulted in freedom from that bondage.

If you have some "housecleaning" to do to create for yourself an environment for success, now might be a good time to note what needs to be done. Determine to choose wisely what you allow into your space, and clean out what's already there that threatens to hinder you from moving forward into more positive self-talk.

From Negative to Positive

On the one hand, we are not to think of ourselves more highly than we should (Rom. 12:3). On the other hand, we are to learn to appreciate who God made us to be, our distinct and unique appearances, our intellects and capabilities, even our family lines. And we need to talk to ourselves accordingly.

You are a spirit with a soul living in the body God gave you, fully loaded with gifts, talents, a personality style that's just yours, and one life to live here on planet Earth. If someone else's words tear you down, use your own words to build yourself up!

King David, one of the most prominent characters in the Bible, not only talked to himself but also knew what to do when he felt despair. He says:

> Why, my soul, are you downcast?
> Why so disturbed within me?

> Put your hope in God,
>> for I will yet praise him,
>> my Savior and my God. (Ps. 43:5)

To walk in freedom from hurting words—even those we speak to ourselves—perhaps we could take a lesson from this king.

In chapter 8, we will explore our unique differences and how those differences are related to words we hear and speak. Before we do, consider the following questions in evaluating your own self-talk.

it's **your** turn

1. When you look in your mirror, what do you see in each of the five categories listed earlier in this chapter?

   Physical appearance:

   Intellect:

   Capabilities:

   Position in life:

   Family line:

2. What words do you most find yourself speaking to the image in the mirror?

3. If the words you speak to yourself are negative, can you trace them to someone who spoke those words to you? If so, who said them and why do you think they were spoken?

4. Knowing you have the authority to break the power of negative words spoken to you by yourself, consider the following prayer:

Father God, I break the power of the words I have spoken to myself, words that say I _____
(fill in the blank with your negative self-talk)*, and I choose to speak only words that edify, uplift, and give life to myself. In Jesus's name, I pray, amen.*

8

fearfully and
wonderfully made

> To be yourself in a world that is constantly trying to make you
> something else is the greatest accomplishment.
>
> RALPH WALDO EMERSON

No matter our beliefs, our countries of origin, our culture or race, you and I have the same Creator who says to us in His written love letter—the Scriptures—that we are fearfully and wonderfully made, woven together in the wombs of our mothers, and born into this world for such a time as this. There's no getting around that if you believe as I do that the Bible is the infallible and inerrant Word of almighty God.

Yes, there are those who argue otherwise, that the Bible is a book of myths and strange stories, but when it comes to the beginning of life, no matter what the baby is called and when, there seems to be no argument regarding how new life begins and where.

Basically, when the sperm of a man makes its way into the fallopian tube of a woman and that single sperm meets up with a woman's egg cell, they combine with half the DNA from the man (father) and half the DNA from the woman (mother) to become a new person. If this was all we had to say about the beginning of life, that in itself is a miracle. What happens in the next thirty-eight or so weeks before the baby is born merely amplifies the miraculous.

What little I know about how the human body works, I can tell you it had to be a supreme being, a master planner, who created something as intricate and sophisticated as the human body. I am not some casual happenstance, and neither are you.

The purpose of this chapter is not to prove anyone right or wrong, nor is it to argue one theory against another. My aim is to show how unique and exquisite you and I are. We talked about this in chapter 4, but I want to go a little deeper into what makes us distinctively different, one-of-a-kind human beings.

If we can get a handle on just how special and unique we all are, and if we can learn to recognize and appreciate our differences, we can better understand (1) what makes each of us tick, (2) why we react and respond to certain stimuli, especially spoken words, and (3) why we say and do what we do. And all this despite what others might say or think or even what we perceive about ourselves.

In chapter 4, we talked about how different we are from one another, even if we're a twin. So just what is it that makes us so dissimilar? And why does it matter?

Let's answer the second question first. It matters because creating and maintaining good, healthy relationships depend on knowing and understanding our differences. If I understand my unique traits and you understand yours, we can operate out of who we are instead of who we think we need to be. The same holds true for understanding the personality styles and gifts of those we spend most of our time with and of those we see only occasionally.

When we understand each other's unique styles, I can allow room for you to be you and you can allow room for me to be me. It will eliminate the need for us to know who's right and who's wrong on certain matters. And it will help clear up why particular words were spoken, or not.

Of the several personality assessments and evaluations in both the spiritual and the secular realm, and there are many good tests, we will focus on only three: the four DISC personality styles, the seven spiritual motivational gifts, and the five love languages.

You might be asking why. This is a book about the effects of spoken words, right? Yes, but knowing how we individually operate, so to speak, gives us clear indicators of how and why we respond or react in a variety of circumstances, why we say the things we do, and how we respond to the words of others.

Shortly, we will explore these assessments in more depth, but first here's a quick example of what the three assessments combined might look like. In the DISC personality-style assessment, I am primarily a "D." That means I am results-oriented and interested in the bottom line. A spiritual motivational gift I assess high in is that of "teacher," and "words of affirmation" are prominent on my list of love languages.

So if I'm having a conversation with someone, based on the traits in these three assessments, I can turn a casual chat between friends into a results-driven teaching with tons of encouragement. That's all well and good, but if I'm not careful I can appear to be preachy and overly dramatic.

Now let's look at how I might react or respond based on how I process words spoken to me. Since my personality style, motivational gifts, and love language are now acting as filters, I'm more inclined to better receive (1) words that deliver the bottom line, (2) facts over fluff, and (3) uplifting words as opposed to negativity. Would you gather that I'm a relatively serious but positive person?

Over the years, it has been suggested that I lighten up. I'm sure my earliest surroundings have a lot to do with my seriousness. There was not a lot of frivolity in my household. But now I see that my solemnness also comes from the gifts God wove throughout my fabric when He knit me together in my mother's womb. I came equipped to be a bottom-line person who likes to teach and who enjoys the positive over the negative.

And you came equipped with certain gifts and traits as well. If you don't already know yours, do yourself a favor and find out. Once you do, things you never understood about yourself will come to light. You'll have a better feel for why you do the things you do and say the things you say. And it's okay! You are uniquely you, loved and delighted in by the One who made you just the way you are. You no longer need to strive to become someone you are not.

I have no doubt there's room for me to lighten up. But now I see it as something I can work on and not a rebuke of who I am. I can't help the way I was created. My maker and Creator drew up the plan for me. I no longer have to look in the mirror and say to myself, "Mary, you are way too serious. Lighten up, girl!" Quite honestly, what others might see as frivolous and funny, I sometimes don't, and I now have confidence enough in who God made me to be to feel okay with that.

Who's got time for all this? You do and so do I. If we want to be better communicators, both as receivers and contributors of words, we need to better understand ourselves and those around us. Spouses should know the traits of each other. Parents should know those of their children. Friends would do well to know them of one another. Coworkers too.

It's not all that complicated. And once you've studied just a little on what these qualities are, you'll begin to recognize them in yourself and others.

Here's a little caveat. Suppose your spouse or coworker or friend isn't interested in finding out about themselves (or you, for that matter). That makes no difference. If you take the time to bone up on these things about yourself, they will greatly improve your own communication skills, and you'll be less apt to become offended. To be equipped not to become offended is a tremendous goal.

Now let's look, one by one, at the three areas of assessment. I hope you find this study as fascinating as I do.

What Makes You You and Me Me?

The first assessment we'll discuss is the *DISC Personality Style*. Briefly, here are what the four letters stand for:

D = Dominant. This style sees the big picture, is interested primarily in the bottom line, and makes decisions rather quickly.

I = Influencer. Often the life of the party, this style loves
   to socialize and is fun loving. They make decisions
   quickly as well.

S = Servant or Steady. Those who possess this style are
   family oriented. They like to serve others, and they
   take their time to make decisions.

C = Conscientious. These people love details. They
   thrive on information, and they tend to take a lot of
   time in their decision-making.

Here's an example of what communication can look like
between someone with a D personality (me) and someone
with a C personality (my husband).

One Saturday morning, Bob took our car to a body shop
guy who works weekends in his home garage. We needed
to see if he could fix a small dent in our right front bumper.

When Bob returned, I was working on my laptop at the
dining room table. Bob joined me and proceeded to tell me
about John, the body shop guy. He told me about the kind
of work he does, the family he comes from, his siblings, his
mom and dad, his country of origin, his desires to go to college, and on and on. You see, Bob knows no strangers. Often,
his conversations with someone new turn into interviews.
And Bob loves relating his findings to me.

The more Bob talked, the more I felt hot and agitated. I
changed positions in my chair. And I knew my countenance
had to be indicating I was not fully involved in my side of the
conversation, that of listening. Midway into Bob's detailed
account of John and his family, I wrote a note on a pad of
paper next to my computer.

At last, Bob said, "Oh, and John did what he could to fix the car and didn't charge us anything."

Stone-faced, I asked if I could read something to him. He said, "Sure."

I picked up the pad of paper and read: "His C is driving my D crazy." He had a quizzical look on his face, a most natural reaction. Then I explained.

I told him that in my research for this book I came across some notes from my direct-marketing days. One of our extensive trainings was the DISC personality styles. I reminded Bob that I'm a high D, a bottom-line kind of gal, and he's a high C, someone more interested in details.

Immediately, he responded, "Ah, you would rather I had started out by saying, 'John fixed the car and didn't charge us anything.'"

"Bingo!" I said. Yes, I just wanted to know if the car was fixed and how much it cost. It's not that I don't love to hear about other people. I do. And it's not that I'm not interested in hearing what my husband has to say. I am. But sometimes in my conversations with him, I feel like I'm on information overload. I just don't need all the details, especially when I'm waiting for the bottom line.

Here's the bonus. At last, after nearly twenty-five years of marriage, we were able to conclude Bob was neither right nor wrong in his delivery and I wasn't right or wrong in my reaction. It just happens to be our individual and unique styles. Now that we understand our differences, we can embrace the variances and give room for each other to be who we are created to be.

Nowadays when Bob comes home from an outing, he asks what I'd like first, the bottom line or the details. And the great thing is, I'm more receptive to his reports, because I realize details are important to who he is.

Are you a D, I, S, or C? Perhaps in the brief descriptions above, you caught a glimpse of your own unique personality type. What about those of the people closest to you? What about friends and coworkers?

Consider arranging a fun session to work together on discovering your styles, and then discuss your findings with one another. I can almost guarantee you will not only appreciate knowing your individual style or styles, but you might also find that what bothered you before—maybe even offended you—makes little difference now.

Why We Do What We Do

Another powerful assessment in knowing how to improve communication skills is our *spiritual motivational gifts* listed in Romans 12:6–8:

> Since we have gifts that differ according to the grace given to us, each of us is to exercise them accordingly: if prophecy, according to the proportion of his faith; if service, in his serving; or he who teaches, in his teaching; or he who exhorts, in his exhortation; he who gives, with liberality; he who leads, with diligence; he who shows mercy, with cheerfulness. (NASB)

So then, the seven gifts are prophecy, serving, teaching, exhortation, giving, leading, and mercy.

Interestingly, both Bob and I assess high in leading and teaching. We are also firstborns. Can you imagine the struggle from time to time in our interactions with one another? Can you imagine one leader trying to communicate a message to another leader? Or one teacher to another teacher? Thankfully, over the years, we have learned how to offer grace.

I strongly encourage you to go online and take both the DISC and the motivational gifts assessment if you don't already know your unique style and gifts. There are many other tests available, but I believe these two will tell you volumes about yourself and about those with whom you spend considerable time.

As in our personality styles, what's important to remember about gifts is that it's not a matter of who is right and who is wrong. If there's anything right or wrong, it's in knowing someone's unique traits and not allowing them to be who they are and/or in not accommodating their styles for better communication.

Find out what your motivational gifts are and then learn about their related traits. Walk freely and confidently in your gifts, but also walk responsibly. God did not give us these gifts to turn people off but rather to totally and equally—together—accomplish His kingdom work.

Lana Heightley is founder and president of Women With A Mission, and for years she has taken missions teams around the world. Understanding the importance of the motivational gifts and how they relate to one another, she wrote the book *Presents from on High*.[1] It's a fascinating study.

While Lana wrote her book so that women could understand their own significance and uniqueness as they uncover their spiritual DNA, her book speaks to everyone, since we all are motivated by one or more of these gifts with one or two being dominant. Briefly, they are as follows:

Those with the gift of *prophecy* proclaim God's truth without compromise. They quickly discern spiritual issues. And they exhibit a strong will.

Those who *serve* love to meet people's practical needs and they step right in, often without being asked.

Teachers enjoy research, learning, and instructing others. They emphasize accuracy. And more often than not, they see things in black and white.

Encouragers love to exhort others and counsel those in need; to them talking comes easy.

Givers want to meet the needs of ministry. They joyfully give materially and financially. And they often have a keen propensity for business.

Leaders are able to organize others to achieve a common goal. They see the big picture. And they exhibit strong administrative skills.

Those with the gift of *mercy* have compassion for those who are suffering mentally, physically, or emotionally. They're long-suffering, sympathetic, and empathetic.

Do you recognize yourself in any of these brief descriptions? How about those you spend time with, such as family members, friends, or coworkers? Can you see how the various gifts can affect how you each respond to certain situations—and spoken words?

Let's paint a picture or two. Let's say you're a teacher, like I am, and you're in a conversation with a friend who is not. You're having a nice chat over a cup of coffee, and then you go into teaching mode. I can talk about this because I've done it.

In fact, I've apologized afterward for taking a simple and fun conversation and turning it into a lesson, applying Scripture verses and anecdotes to support my points.

Can you see where my gift could get in the way of a relationship, whether casual or intimate? My words could be perceived as highfalutin, know-it-all, even judgmental to the person on the other side of the conversation.

Do you understand why it might be important to know your own and others' motivational gifts when it comes to spoken words?

According to Lana's book, here are some other ways our gifts can be misunderstood:

Perceivers can wonder why others don't see spiritual things the way they do and may even accuse others of compromising.

Servers have a hard time when others don't automatically respond to the needs of others.

Encouragers just want everyone to get along and are critical when others don't extend enough grace.

Teachers, expecting things to be done systematically, have difficulty listening to someone with a nonteaching gift try to explain or teach them something.

Administrators can't understand why everyone else can't see the needs that must be addressed and in an orderly way in order to reach a common goal.

Contributors tend to evaluate the worth of others by what they give in time, money, and resources and often are put out if others don't naturally give as much as they do.

Mercy givers can't comprehend why everyone isn't more sensitive to the feelings of others.

Can you see how misunderstandings, even words of ridicule or anger, could come into play? Can you see how someone might feel and even hold on to resentment, bitterness, and anger when what was really going on was that someone was operating in their motivational gift? Can you see how negative self-talk could result?

Take time to assess your motivational gifts if you're sincere in wanting to better understand yourself and others. Make the most of your conversations, and perhaps most importantly, work diligently to keep from being offended and not to offend others.

How We Know We Are Loved

Having seen the play and movie versions, I was excited when I stumbled upon and was able to purchase the book *Fiddler on the Roof*. I never tire of the part where the main character, Tevye, asks his wife, Golde, if she loves him. "Do I what?" Golde replies incredulously. Golde then lists all the practical ways he should get the picture after twenty-five years of marriage. After all, if that doesn't prove her love, what will?

Tevye is relentless in his pursuit. "But do you love me?"[2]

Bob and I play this game from time to time. I will ask him if he loves me. He will say something like, "I washed the dishes, didn't I?" "Yes, but do you love me?" I ask again. Teasingly, he will come up with something else he's done, such as taking out the trash. Finally, we get around to a more serious response.

Here's the thing. Not only do we want to know we are loved, but we also have certain ways that make us feel loved. Gary Chapman, in his book *The 5 Love Languages*,[3] maintains there are five ways through which we offer and receive love: acts of service, words of affirmation, gifts, quality time, and physical touch.

All are quite self-explanatory, and generally we can figure out our preferred language by observing what we do to show love, since we will extend our affection in the way we like to be shown affection. Again, why is this important? Sometimes the greatest things we say to one another are conveyed without speaking a word. Rather, they're shown through our actions, which say, "What's important to you matters to me," especially if that other person is a spouse, family member, or close friend.

Our personality styles, our motivational gifts, and our love languages are only three areas that reveal our individuality. We haven't begun to discuss our unique cultural differences, our special talents and skills, our dreams and callings, or our birth orders. Yes, we are oh so different. And once we understand ourselves a little more, embrace our unique qualities, and appreciate who we and who others are, we can more readily enjoy life and walk out our destinies in peace and delight—and less offended.

If on your journey through life you have not already grasped that you are fearfully and wonderfully created, I pray you soon will. If words from others have left you feeling unworthy, unwanted, and, ultimately, unloved, remember that God in His infinite love for you not only miraculously wove you together in your mother's womb but also wove you together with purpose and with a plan no one else on this earth can complete. It's yours and yours alone to pursue and accomplish by using your unique personality style, motivational gifts, love language, and a myriad of other special traits, preferences, and tendencies that all add up to say there is no one else in the world just like you.

it's **your** turn

1. As you think about the miraculous human body, what aspect of our physical makeup amazes you the most?

2. From what you read in this chapter about the DISC personality styles, which would you say is your dominant style and why?

3. What would you say is high on your list of spiritual motivational gifts and love languages?

4. If you've been able to determine your unique personality style, motivational gifts, and love language from reading this chapter, what about yourself do you better understand?

9

freedom from negative self-talk

Fix your thoughts on what is true and good and right. . . . Think about all you can praise God for and be glad about.

PHILIPPIANS 4:8 TLB

After reading chapter 8 and perhaps discovering your unique and special traits, I hope you're encouraged to speak to yourself more gently and positively, especially since, though the numbers vary, research indicates that while most people speak at a rate of 150 to 200 words per minute, the internal dialogues we carry on are more like 1,300 words per minute.[1] At that rate, if we are not speaking kindly to ourselves, there's the potential for a vast amount of negativity going on in our minds daily.

In some respects, self-talk can be even more damaging than the words of others. Why? Because at the rate of over a thousand words per minute, our self-talk is constant. Day by day, hour by hour, moment by moment, words go through our minds, and most of those words make up what we say to ourselves. We may be reiterating what others have said, but whether the words we speak are original to ourselves or we are repeating the words of others, we are doing it almost all our waking moments.

Six Steps to Freedom

To live happier—and healthier—lives, we really do need to find ways to eliminate negative self-talk. In this chapter, we're going to talk about six of those ways. I'm sure there are more. Let's get started.

Step 1: Embrace Your Uniqueness

Whether it's your personality style, your motivational gifts, your love language, or whatever it is you see in the mirror, appreciate *you* and thank God for making you into the special one-of-a-kind creation you are. Begin to see yourself the way God sees you.

Just as you need to protect yourself from the words of others, you may need to protect yourself from your own words. Others don't have the right to disrespect the sanctity of your life. Neither do you.

Learn to love yourself in a healthy way, God's way. Spend time in His Word and He will guide and direct you in appreciating who you are. He'll also show you ways to develop your special style.

If your self-esteem is too damaged from an abundance of negative input, you may need to spend extra time building yourself up. But do so always in relation to who you are and what the Lord would want you to say and do.

In no way am I suggesting we construct a Pollyanna kind of bubble around ourselves and build ourselves up in an unhealthy way. I'm not saying that we need to think more highly of ourselves than we should. In fact, Scripture is clear we are to esteem others more highly than ourselves (Phil. 2:3).

Honestly, because of the fall of man, besides being uniquely created with special gifts, talents, and callings, we are, at the same time, needy and imperfect. Thankfully, Jesus came to make up for all that.

When we choose to be one of His disciples (to learn of and from Him and to walk in His ways), God looks at us through the filter of His perfect Son, who gave His life for each and every one of us. Will we all respond to His love, mercy, and gift of grace? God surely wants that for us, for He says that He desires that no one perish but wants all to come to repentance and to the saving knowledge of His Son (2 Pet. 3:9; 1 Tim. 2:4). Those of us who do enter that relationship can come to the Father, having been washed in the blood of Christ and cleansed from all our unrighteousness (1 John 1:7, 9). And he who the Son sets free is free indeed (John 8:36). Free from what? Condemnation from others—and from ourselves—and free to embrace our unique differences.

Step 2: Let Go of Your Past

The past is often filled with regrets. Frank Sinatra, a popular singer in the 1940s, sang about living life his way. "Ol' Blue

Eyes" said he had regrets, but they were too few to mention. Not so with me. Mine are too numerous to mention. And from time to time, memories surface that take me back to exact times and places. It might be in a relationship, in my parenting, in missed opportunities, and the list goes on.

I'd like to be able to say that due to my freedom in Christ and my years of "living and learning," I no longer have to deal with regrets. But since I do, I've found ways to deal with them when they return to haunt me. Maybe you'll find these methods helpful as well.

One of the ways I deal with regrets is by taking my thoughts captive, which means to take control of thoughts that resurface. When thoughts had control over me, I found myself spending way too much time wallowing and whining, wishing I could live those times of regret over and do life differently. But the reality is, I can't. When those thoughts return now, I might give them a moment of my time, but then I make the deliberate choice to leave regret where it belongs—in the past—and to move on.

My friend Janie and I spent a writers' weekend together recently. Sharing a car ride to and from, being roommates, and eating our meals together provided ample time to bond more personally. We found ourselves sharing from our pasts and commiserating over our regrets. In her gorgeous North Carolina accent, Janie summed it up for both of us when she said, "Mary, what it boils down to is, if we'd known better, we'd done better." Do I still wish I could change some things? I sure do. But since I can't, I choose to move on and do better in my todays and tomorrows.

Another way I deal with regrets is through expressive writing. This is the type of writing Bob taught the seniors at the assisted-living residence we talked about in chapter 1. Expressive writing, when done regularly and over a period of time, has been shown to improve health and happiness, change destructive life patterns, and bring emotional healing. I urge you to go online and investigate this method on your own. For now, I offer some tips for expressive writing, adapted from the man who discovered this form of therapy, Dr. James Pennebaker.

First, ask yourself if you need to write. That is, do you find yourself thinking about something too much, dreaming about it, or obsessing about it?

Second, plan to write for a minimum of fifteen minutes for three or four days.

Third, do not edit yourself. Don't worry about spelling, grammar, and format. This writing is for your eyes only.

Fourth, plan on destroying what you've written. Whether or not you do destroy it is another matter. Writing as though you are will eliminate inhibitions.[2]

I've done expressive writing. It works!

To live happy and healthy lives today and into our futures, we must be willing to leave our yesterdays where they belong. We need to learn to appreciate and enjoy each new day. And we need to focus on a future filled with purpose and satisfaction.

Step 3: Set Personal Boundaries

Just as we sometimes need to say no to others, there will be times we need to say no to ourselves, especially if something is detrimental to our well-being and causes us to revert to negative self-talk. For example, saying no to comparing ourselves with others, whether on social media, in our circle of friends, or at our workplace. Whenever we compare ourselves with someone else, we will always come up lacking. That's just the way our minds work.

We may have to say no to social media. Oh no, not that! A recent article on forbes.com cites six ways social media affects our mental health. First, social media is addictive. Second, it triggers more sadness and less well-being. Third, we find ourselves comparing our lives with others, which is mentally unhealthy. Fourth, it can lead to jealousy. Fifth, we can get caught in the delusion that getting on social media will be helpful. Sixth, because we have a lot of friends on social media doesn't mean we're more social.[3] I'd like to add a seventh reason to say no to social media. It has the potential to wreak havoc on—even destroy—relationships.

There are obviously some great aspects of social media, but I have found if I'm not careful, I start doing the C word: *comparing*. Here's what Pastor Steven Furtick says about comparing ourselves with others, especially with those on social media: "The reason we struggle with insecurity is because we compare our behind-the-scenes with everyone else's highlight reel."[4] Oh yes!

I've also found social media to be a major peace and time stealer. For example, for eight days straight, I began my early mornings by opening to Facebook and checking on my beloved Sonoma County in Northern California, mainly the town of Santa Rosa, where Bob and I lived and worked early in our marriage. It was burning up, literally. In unprecedented flames, lives, homes, and businesses were being lost to the grotesque monster that came upon its unsuspecting victims in the middle of the night on October 10, 2017, and raged for several more days.

Previous to this, while waiting for enough daylight to walk down to pick up Molly for our morning stroll, I often did a quick check on any emails that might have come in late the previous night and then a quick check of Facebook. Who am I trying to kid? There's never just a quick check of Facebook, at least not for me.

On the morning of October 10, while attempting my quick check of Facebook, I saw a familiar name and face from our days in Santa Rosa. Her post merely read, "Evacuation for some areas of the city." *Evacuation? Why?* I looked in some of the comments and saw the word *fire.* So I did an online search of "Santa Rosa and fire." And then I saw it. Already, by the time I checked, which was 6:30 a.m. EST and 3:30 California time, many were being evacuated from their homes in areas all too familiar to me, areas in which we had lived in the mid-1990s.

I remember thinking, *This can't be. Beautiful Santa Rosa and surrounding areas; surely the damage will be minimal.* For hours, I sat glued to my computer, searching sites, searching others' posts, searching until my head began to feel like it would burst.

What next? I wondered. It seemed like Hurricane Harvey, which had pounded Houston and surrounding areas with flooding the previous August, had set off a series of calamities around the country and beyond that felt never-ending: hurricanes, shootings, terrorist attacks, friends and family members experiencing major life challenges. It seemed as though it was one thing after another, and I began taking it all to heart.

And now the fires in Santa Rosa. It left me feeling help-less and burdened. All this at a time when I was pushing my deadline to get this book written. Suddenly, one morning, I realized these events added up to one huge distraction. Some things could be put on the back burner while I checked social media and all that was going on in the world; the completion of this book was not one of them.

So I chose to say no to myself. On day nine following the outbreak of the fires, as much as I wanted to check on my friends in Northern California and see that the fires were even more contained than they were the day before, I knew one quick glance would lead to several more, and an hour if not many would slip by. I had already lost a lot of writing time. In addition, I'd lost my sense of peace and well-being.

Depressed and in a funk, I had to clear my mind. I decided to list everything I was concerned about—all the calamities, here and abroad, threatening to steal my time and joy. That morning, my expressive writing took the form of a long list. And while I could not do a thing to correct, alleviate, or help in any of the situations, I did the one thing I could do. I lifted my list in prayer to the Lord and placed all my concerns in His able and loving hands. And then I returned to my work on this book.

Did I not love my friends out West and wish for their well-being? Oh yes. Did I not feel remorse for those who lost their homes and all their belongings? Of course, I did. But I had to put it all into God's hands and grab hold of the promise that He would bring beauty from the ashes of these monstrous flames (Isa. 61:3).

I love social media, as many of you do. What a wonderful way to keep in touch with those I cannot see on a regular basis. But again, it can steal too much of my time and peace of mind. This, like everything else, calls for balance and a "no" from time to time.

Step 4: Sing a New Song

But I'm not a singer, you may be saying. Actually, we all sing a song. Put together all the words you say in a day, and you will begin to recognize a certain tempo and theme. The tempo or rhythm might be upbeat. On the other hand, it could sound like a funeral dirge. It might resonate with joy, or it could display extreme sadness. If you don't know the rhythm of the song you're singing, ask a trusted friend or family member to give you honest and constructive feedback.

How about the overarching theme or refrain of your song? Does it reflect forward movement on your part, or are you stuck in a certain area of your life? Again, if you can't objectively assess the accumulated message from the song you're singing, seek out sound advice and then determine to write new lyrics to your life song if necessary. The personal and relational benefits will amaze you.

Step 5: Get into Community

We humans are wired for relationship. From the beginning, God told Adam, the first man He created, that it was not good for man to live alone. So from Adam's rib, He created Eve (Gen. 2:22). And this is the first relationship of two human beings—and the first example of community.

From that point on, humankind has come to depend on one another for fellowship, help, enjoyment, and so much more. In addition, community offers counsel and account-ability. Don't try to do life alone.

We moved to Ocala, Florida, in the summer of 2015 to be near our son Alan and his family of six children, and yes, to leave Michigan winters behind. What a blessing now to be able to see our family often. For a time, because we were new to the area, we joined their community of friends. Before long, however, I felt like there was something missing. And then I realized what it was. I needed girlfriends, women around my age and with similar experiences and interests.

Once settled into our new home, I joined a small group at our new church. Then I took a course to become part of the leadership team, which enabled me to begin my own small group for writers. From both small groups, the Lord blessed me with many new friends.

In the case of Adam, God brought the relationship to him. And there's no doubt, He still puts people together. In my case, I felt comfortable taking some initiative. Either way, we are wired for relationship. And as they say at my church, "We are better together!"

Step 6: Serve Others

We may not all have the gift of serving, but there are numerous ways to reach beyond ourselves. I once had the opportunity to encourage a group of women to take what they enjoyed doing and turn it into ministry. An in-class survey revealed we had among us someone who loved to sew. Another enjoyed baking. Still another loved to care for little ones. We had one who loved music and another who spent much time in prayer.

Once we determined what each of us enjoyed doing, we discussed several ways to reach out to others. The woman who loved to sew could make dresses out of pillowcases and ship them to little girls in faraway lands. The baker in our group could make an extra loaf of bread and take it to a shut-in. The one who loved little ones could offer respite to a young mother. The musician could take her gift to a nursing home. The woman who loved to pray could call her neighbors and ask how she could lift them up in prayer.

What do you especially enjoy doing? How could you turn what you love to do into serving others? What better way to get your mind off yourself and reach out to others? Looks like a win-win to me.

Shield of Protection

It doesn't seem like we should need to build a shield of protection *from* ourselves. From others, maybe, but from ourselves? But if we're talking to ourselves almost constantly, then it might be important to have that inner shield as well as the outer shield. How do we do that? Think of these six steps as the components of the shield. As we embrace who we are, choose to let go of our pasts, set personal boundaries, write new lyrics to our life song, get into community, and serve others, we can walk in newness of life—leaving behind negative self-talk and moving forward into all our Creator has for us.

Before we move into part 3, "Words We Speak to Others," take some time to consider the following questions about walking in freedom from your own hurting words.

it's **your** turn

1. After reading this chapter, can you think of ways you can be kinder to yourself? List them here.

2. What personal boundaries might you need to set up for yourself?

3. If the lyrics to the song you're singing need to be changed, what new words would you like to use?

4. What do you enjoy doing that could be used to reach out to others?

words we speak to others

We have a Christian duty to encourage one another. Many a time a word of praise or thanks or appreciation or cheer has kept a man on his feet. Blessed is the man [or woman] who speaks such a word.

WILLIAM BARCLAY

10

life-changing words

A word fitly spoken is like apples of gold in pictures of silver.

PROVERBS 25:11 KJV

From her first year of teaching in an Israeli second grade classroom, Chen Miller tells the story of a little boy with big eyes who cursed, spat, and screamed at her. Calmly, Chen walked over to where he sat and whispered these words: "You have a big heart. You are clever. And I know you're a good boy."

The little boy called her stupid and said she didn't know anything. He told her he was disturbed, and everyone knew it. His teachers and headmaster, even his parents, told him he was disturbed.

Once again, Chen whispered, "You have a big heart. You are clever. And I know you're a good boy." He ran out of the classroom.

The second week of school came, and nothing changed. He still cursed, spat, and screamed at his teacher, to which she repeated her refrain.

The third week, when she walked into her classroom, she saw a little chair sitting next to hers, and in that chair was the little boy with the big eyes. Chen said, "That day he chose me to be his teacher."

Toward the end of the first year, the little boy asked his teacher, "How do you know children are good?"

Chen told him her secret. Until fifth grade, she could not read, write, or connect numbers. She believed she was stupid and had a broken brain. As a student in a special needs class, she was sure nothing good would ever come out of her.

Now she teaches within the same structure that threatened to give up on her. Desiring to help change the system, she reminds educators that the thoughts and words they use about a child will at some stage become the thoughts and words that child will think about himself.[1]

For Such a Time as This

When I first heard the small group's name, "PJ and B," my mind transposed the letters and I quickly came up with peanut butter and jelly. However, PJ and B stands for pajamas and breakfast. And it's the brainchild of a woman by the name of Cassandra at the church I attend.

Breakfast generally consists of an egg casserole, a pastry, and juice, which Cassandra takes to the home of a mother whose young daughter had a slumber party the previous evening. Over the meal, Cassandra gets to know the girls. Following breakfast, she teaches them the story of Queen

Esther, the Bible character who entered history at the precise time God planned to use her to help save the nation of Israel.

Cassandra emphasizes to these young girls that they are so much more than they think they are. She tells them that, like Queen Esther, they are here on earth for a special reason, "for such a time as this" (Esther 4:14). She reinforces their uniqueness and beauty as God's creations. And she encourages them in the gifts and talents God has given each one—for their good and for His glory.

Cassandra's words will echo in the heads and hearts of these young girls as they walk the sometimes difficult paths of life. Will her encouragement be enough to cancel out all the negatives these same girls will hear in their homes, online, in school, and in many other places? It may. Bare minimum, this caring woman's words are seeds planted in the hearts and minds of these young ladies.

People like Chen and Cassandra choose to use their words to change the lives of children for the good. Likewise, there are fine male counterparts offering life-giving words to our young people. What about you and me? How will we use our words? Will we offer words that belittle and wound hearts, or will we offer words that help change lives for the good?

Better or Worse?

It seems a given that we would all want to use our words to change lives for the better, to offer life-giving words. And honestly, I think that's generally your intention and mine. In fact, if someone were to accuse us of hurting them with our words, unless we are malevolent, we'd probably be surprised at their accusation. "What do you mean?" we might ask. "I didn't intend to hurt you."

But just as words have often been spoken to us out of woundedness, we too walk around broken and hurt and quite capable of doing the same to others. Is it any wonder our words will not always be as life giving as we'd like to think they are?

Whether our words are life or death giving, there is one thing we can be sure of. They will leave someone either feeling better or feeling worse. Author and Bible teacher Rick Renner says:

> When we leave a person and a conversation, let's endeavor to leave the fragrance of Christ's love in our wake. Let's make it a goal to leave that conversation knowing that we did our best to get better acquainted with that person's heart and to discover more of the Father's heart for his or her life. Let's deliberately show those we speak with the attention they deserve and leave them wondering why we never have much to say about ourselves. *I think that is what Jesus would do!*[2]

I wish I could say that every time I leave a person, what remains is the sweet aroma of Christ and the person feeling better. Since I'm a more positive person than not and since another of my motivational gifts is that of encouragement, I think that happens much of the time. But sometimes when I've left a conversation, I think, *You talk too much!* Encouragers can be that way. If they also have the motivational gift of teaching, that could spell double trouble, especially for those on the receiving end of the conversation. I know myself and my tendencies, so I need to be careful.

I've observed though that however well-intentioned some people might think they are, not everyone is considerate with their words. I see it everywhere, even in coffee shops. Recently, while writing and enjoying a cup of dark roast, I looked up to see a pregnant woman, perhaps in her thirties, walking over to someone she recognized at a table across from mine. As the ladies chatted, I heard the young mom say she was having a baby girl on Monday.

At another table sat two older women. One looked up when she heard the announcement and asked, "You're having your first?"

"Oh, no, I have an eighteen-month-old," responded the young momma.

The older woman replied, "And you're wanting another one right now?"

Awkwardly and a little dejectedly, the soon-to-deliver momma walked away. If she had said to the woman, "It's none of your business," she would have been justified. It's easy to assess that the woman's words did not leave this young mom feeling better.

Oh, the things that come out of our mouths when it is truly none of our business or when we don't know what to say. Author Paul Miller is quoted as saying, "Never pass up an opportunity to keep your mouth shut."[3] And I would add, especially when you have no stake in the matter.

A Little Bit of Matter Called the Tongue

What is the little critter with the power to do an incredible amount of good or considerable damage? Of course, it's the tongue, that approximately two-ounce, three-inch muscle organ we carry inside our mouths, without which we would have difficulty licking, tasting, swallowing, or articulating words.

Of the fascinating things to know about this relatively small organ in our bodies, the most amazing is the power the tongue has when used to utter words. The Bible tells us that life and death are in the power of the tongue (Prov. 18:21), that with our tongues we can bless our Lord and Father God and curse people who are made in His likeness (James 3:9). While there are more important organs in our bodies in terms of function, such as the heart and liver, no other organ in our bodies is as powerful.

But is it the tongue's fault? If you recall from an earlier chapter, we said the problem is not the tongue. The problem is that the tongue is connected to the heart. Whatever is in the heart will eventually pour out of the mouth. So the words our tongues utter are a direct reflection of what's going on inside us.

I don't know about the woman at the coffee shop that day. I can't determine by her unfeeling question to the young mother exactly what was going on in her heart, but I imagine she is not subtle in a lot of her conversations.

Another coffee shop incident reveals that sometimes we speak out of foolishness—or is it extreme neediness? While waiting for another writer to join me one morning for mutual sharing and encouragement, I couldn't help overhearing a grandmother at a table just a few feet away talking to her granddaughter. She was lavishing praise on the young girl, which is not so unusual. But what bothered me were the words that concluded her admiration: "You know you are the prettiest in your family, don't you? Don't tell your sister I said so. This will be our little secret, just between you and me."

I'm not sure what the grandmother said after that or how the granddaughter responded, because my mind began playing out scenarios that placed this youngster in precarious places, to say the least. I don't know in what birth order this granddaughter fell, but to have someone as prominent in a person's life as a grandmother say something complimentary to her but uncomplimentary about a sibling, whether younger or older, had to leave her feeling confused and uncomfortable.

If this young girl had any animosity or feelings of superiority to her sister, her grandmother's words only served to fuel that flame. If the girl did not feel anything but love and genuine friendship toward her sister, her grandmother's words could make her feel as though she needed to take sides. What foolishness would prompt an adult to put a child in this type of situation? Or was it extreme neediness in the grandmother's life that provoked those words?

Genuine praise and encouragement—yes, by all means, let's lavish both on those we love, for goodness knows they hear enough negativity on any given day. But be careful. First, let's be careful we are not praising our children and grandchildren solely for their physical looks. Too much of that can make them overly self-conscious and sensitive about their appearance. And second, let's not overdo our praise for how they perform. Too much of that can motivate them to strive for approval.

Rather, praise and encourage them for just being who they are, creations of almighty God with gifts and talents and the potential—yes, to do things but more importantly—to bring glory to the Father for just being His magnificent creations.

Just Be

Years ago, God used a friend to mentor me in my faith. One day she asked how she could pray for me. I told her I wanted prayer for what I should be doing next. I didn't want to miss the mark in accomplishing the work God had for me to do.

She replied, "Mary, why do you have to be doing something all the time? Can't you just be?" And then she reminded me that God loves me for me. He was not going to love me more if I did more. And He was not going to withdraw His love if I did less. He already loved me and was pleased with me.

And, readers, He already loves you. "I don't feel it," you say? That does not negate the fact that He loves you. He demonstrated His love when He gave His Son to die on your behalf and mine. He loves us that much. We don't need to do more than go to Him in repentance and receive His gift of grace.

Yes, our doing brings gratification—to us. Yet, often we "do," thinking we are bringing Him satisfaction. When we said yes to His gift, that was satisfaction enough. From then on, He looks down from heaven and says, "There's Mary; she's mine." Replace my name with yours, because He thinks that about you as well.

When I look at my children, I say, "There's Laura, Rob, and Alan; they're mine." Oh, I know they are on loan from the Lord so that I could take part in their raising. But He chose to loan them to me. When I look at my grandchildren, I say, "There's Daniel, Nathan, Timothy, Christina, Andrew, Aaron, Kaitlin, David, Samuel, Annabelle, and Faithlynn; they're mine." They are all gifts from almighty God to cherish and call my own.

Nothing my children and grandchildren do or don't do can make me love them any more or any less. They each have a special place in my heart. Each one, created in the image of God, has gifts, talents, interests, and callings, which I pray they use to bring satisfaction to themselves and glory to God. If they do, I love them. If they don't, I love them. Not because of what they do but because of who they are.

To say to one of my grandchildren that she or he is prettier or more handsome, smarter, or more talented than any of the rest is a recipe for disaster, to say the least.

Be Careful Little Ears What You Hear

Cindy had an unusual childhood. Raised mostly around adults, she always felt more comfortable at the dining room table, where the grown-ups gathered for coffee.

Cindy's mother and father often fought, and Cindy could count on conversations around the table eventually centering on her father's most recent transgressions. Her mother's friends had become her refuge, her sounding board.

But I suspect Cindy looked at her dad as her hero as most little girls do. How could her mom talk about him like that? Often, Cindy withdrew into her own little world, becoming quiet and thoughtful and feeling quite alone.

It was during those formative years that Cindy determined she would never talk about her dad like her mother did. And she would never be a complainer. Good traits to develop, right? Don't talk bad about someone and don't grumble, which was all well and good until it was taken to the extreme and became a way of covering up. Cindy not only refrained from saying derogatory things about her father and his waywardness, but, when she married, she also did not share with anyone the indiscretions of her young husband. For years, Cindy kept everything inside and behind closed doors. No one knew of her unhappiness and despair. Cindy was good at covering up, not only for her dad but also for the man she married. Without realizing it and certainly with no intention of doing so, Cindy's mother set up her daughter for years of heartache and remorse.

When the story of her failed marriage finally emerged, Cindy's shocked and stunned friends were speechless. Under the impression that all was well in Cindy's household, she was the one they went to for support when they had issues in their own homes.

This section is titled "Be Careful Little Ears What You Hear." Perhaps it should be "Be Careful Adult Mouths What You Speak." Children are not responsible for what they hear, especially youngsters who don't know how to avoid what's being spoken in their midst. In fact, they don't know how to avoid what's being spoken within earshot, even if it's behind closed doors. It's easy for children, or anyone for that matter, to hear bits and pieces of conversations and hang their thoughts and conclusions on those words, not realizing that what was said may not concern them at all or may be out of context.

Adults, and I'm speaking to myself as well, let's be careful to keep our negative thoughts to ourselves, and let's be aware of what our little ones might hear. Just as in Cindy's example, words can leave their impressions for years, if not lifetimes, and can unsuspectingly promote unhealthy lifestyles and relationships.

A young mom I know does something extraordinary on a regular basis with one of her daughters, who often operates out of her emotions. At bedtime, to help clear up any wrong thinking on her daughter's part, the wise momma quizzes her little girl to find out if she is carrying any offenses from that day, something she might have heard or thought that made her feel bad. What wisdom on this mother's part. Imagine the peace we might all enjoy if we were to regularly follow her example with our own family members.

A Change of Heart

It was tempting to include in this chapter a long list of Scripture verses that talk about the tongue and the power of our words, such as "The tongue has the power of life and death" (Prov. 18:21) or "A gentle answer turns away wrath" (Prov. 15:1 NASB) or "Pleasant words are a honeycomb, sweet to the soul and healing to the bones" (Prov. 16:24 NASB).

We could commit to memorizing the verses, even doing everything in our power to take them to heart and live by them. And perhaps we should. But unless we have a change of heart, a healing of our broken places, and unless we take care not to talk out of weariness, disappointments, and hopelessness, all the memorization in the world and all the commitment we can muster will mean nothing. It will be business as usual in our everyday lives. Nothing changes if nothing changes.

The tongue has the capacity to speak the words, but the heart is instructing the tongue what to say. It's really about cause and effect, which is the theory that an action or event will produce a certain response to the action in the form of another event. A healed heart, or at least one being transformed by the power of God, will most often issue words of life. A broken, embittered, or damaged heart—a heart still in need of much repair—will respond in the form of hurtful words to someone else and maybe to oneself in the form of self-talk.

Because the tongue has the power to offer life or death, based on the condition of our hearts, Scripture teaches us to bridle the tongue. Just as we might put a bridle on a horse to control the horse, we are to rein in our tongues to gain control of what we speak (James 3:3–5). The same is true when we ask the Lord to put a guard over our mouths (Ps. 141:3). We are asking Him to help us gain control over what we say so as not to sin with our mouths in the form of harmful and negative words to and about others or to ourselves. To do that, we must submit to the Lord and listen for His leading. Sometimes this will come in what is called a check in our spirits. We get ready to say something but sense a little impression inside us that feels like a warning. At times, I am happy to say, I have given heed to that warning, stopping midsentence. Other times I have not and have been sorry afterward for my words.

Ecclesiastes 3:7 tells us there is a time to be silent and a time to speak. If we're going to err on one side or the other, let's choose to err on the side of keeping silent.

Even in Passing, Words Have Power

Years ago, I volunteered at a crisis pregnancy center. A couple of years after I had moved on, I received an email from another volunteer saying a DJ from a local radio station called and asked for me. She told him I was no longer there, and he told the receptionist, "Well, this is a somewhat personal matter, but I will share it with you, if I may."

He gave her his name and said, "I was speaking with Mary one day when at the end of our phone conversation she said, 'God bless you.' No one had *ever* said that to me before in my entire life. I sit here right now with my Bible open because of her."

He went on to say he had been raised in another faith, but he was not strong in his beliefs and had never owned a Bible. "After what Mary said, I wanted a Bible, and even thought of taking a Gideon's from a motel room." With a chuckle, he said he figured there are some things you just don't do. "Then I saw my boss reading his Bible. One thing led to another, and he bought me a Bible." The caller then asked the volunteer to pass along a message to me: "God bless you, Mary."

I'm embarrassed to say that in the past, I often spoke those words, "God bless you," to others somewhat routinely, as a way to end a conversation. When I say them now, I mean them sincerely and am reminded that our words do matter, even in passing.

When Encouraging, Just Encourage

We began this chapter talking about the encouraging words of women like Chen and Cassandra. It seems fitting to end in a similar fashion.

Many books have been written on the topic of encouragement. One of my favorites is *Unleashing the Power of Encouragement* by Reid Lamport. I could quote many things from his book, but I'll simply share a story from his chapter titled "Encouraging by Way of Omission."

Reid tells about a lady in his neighborhood who walked by his home one day while he was on a ladder doing some gutter work. She said to him, "Your landscaping is beautiful." He was grateful for her compliment and thanked her.

When Reid completed his task and went to put away his ladder, he was reminded of his cluttered garage. In fact, he said the sight of it was almost overwhelming. His neighbor could have said something like, "Your landscaping is beautiful; however, you might want to keep that garage door down," and he would not have blamed her. But she didn't. Reid said, "Had she mentioned the state of the garage, even in a joking manner, her encouragement concerning the yard would have been nullified."[4] And Reid would have completed his task feeling defeated rather than uplifted.

How about you? Can you think of times when someone has complimented you but then tacked on a condition? For example, "Great job! But you might want to do it a little differently next time." Unfortunately, the sentiment behind the words "Great job!" was negated by the admonition to do it differently in the future.

We've all heard these kinds of statements: "All As on your report card and only one B, wonderful! Next semester though let's shoot for all As" or "You played that song beautifully. But the last couple of measures could have been a little smoother." And chances are, we've said similar things to others.

There will be appropriate times for teaching, admonishing, and correcting, but not when our aim is to bolster, encourage, or lift someone's spirits. When your desire is to encourage, watch out for words such as *but, yet, though, however, except*. Reid writes, "I'm not trying to say we should never rebuke someone; I'm just saying it shouldn't be on the coattails of a word of encouragement."[5] When encouraging, let's stick to encouraging.

it's **your** turn

1. Who in your life would benefit from hearing words of encouragement and affirmation? How will you deliver those words today or in the near future?

2. Think of the last time you got together with a friend. How would you describe how they felt about themselves when you parted? What might you do in the future to ensure that those you meet with feel better about themselves once you've stepped away?

3. Have you felt in the past that the more you do for the Lord, the more He's going to love you? After reading this chapter, how do you feel?

4. Since we all benefit from being unconditionally complimented, what steps can you take to extend that courtesy to others?

11

seeking the forgiveness
of others

Forgiveness is the best form of love. It takes a strong person
to say sorry and an even stronger person to forgive.

UNKNOWN

From my own experience and that of people I've spoken with and read about, there is a consensus that it's much easier to extend forgiveness to someone than to seek the forgiveness of others. To ask can be awkward and embarrassing, and it can place those of us who feel the need to seek forgiveness in places of extreme vulnerability. But make no mistake, doing so is a necessary component of healthy relationships.

To simplify our understanding of what it looks like to ask forgiveness of another, let's once again use the 5 Ws and H approach.

Who needs to ask for forgiveness? At some time or another, we all need to seek the forgiveness of others.

What do we need to ask forgiveness for? For the things we've said and done, whether intentional or not, that have hurt or offended another person.

Where do we ask for forgiveness from another? Most often in privacy, but there may be times when asking in public is beneficial, perhaps even required.

When do we ask for forgiveness? The sooner the better, when we know we've offended someone.

Why do we need to ask for forgiveness? Just as others have offended us and we need to release them from their offenses, we too need to be released from offenses we have committed.

How do we ask for forgiveness? There are a variety of ways. But let's take first things first.

Recognizing the Need

Becoming aware of our need to ask for someone's forgiveness is the first step. At times, it will be as obvious as the nose on your face. But at other times, you may not have a clue. Oh, you might feel a coolness or distance, and you might suspect something is wrong, but the other person can act as if everything is just fine while harboring something deep and wide.

Such is the case of a resident we will call Dora in the same assisted-living residence as Marilyn in chapter 1. The same day Marilyn shared her story with Bob in his writing class about the classmate who wouldn't share a swing, Dora spoke up about something her sister, also in the class, said to her over seventy years ago.

Mystified, Dora's sister had no remembrance of what she supposedly said seven decades earlier that still affected her younger sister. All those years, Dora acted as though everything was just fine while holding deep within words she perceived as negative and hurtful. Obviously, the sisters had something to discuss. It's possible that what Dora heard those many years ago and took to heart are words her sister actually spoke. We can only hope they came to some resolution and level of healing.

It's also possible that what Dora heard was not at all what was spoken or implied. Sometimes our perceptions are incorrect.

In his book *The Gift of Forgiveness*, Dr. Charles Stanley tells about an experience with his son, Andy, when Andy, in his early teens, discovered he had musical talents and began playing the piano by ear. Dr. Stanley says that everything his son pounded out on the piano sounded the same. One day he stuck his head in the living room where his son was playing and said, "Andy, is that all you know?" Andy stopped playing immediately and never again played when his parents were in the house.

Some years later, when Andy was in his twenties, Dr. Stanley said one of their conversations turned toward music. Andy then confessed that when his father said those words to him all those many years ago, he took it as rejection and began to resent his father. Dr. Stanley said, "He was too young to understand that my comment was directed at his music, not at him as my son. And I was too insensitive to understand that the budding young artist saw little distinction between his work and his personhood."

What caused Andy's reaction and subsequent resentment toward his father was perceived rejection, because as Dr. Stanley writes, "I did not intend to reject him."[1] His son's response, though, was the same as if it had been intentional.

Acting on the Need

You've determined your need to ask someone for forgiveness. Hard though the process may seem, what steps can you take to make amends? Here are a few.

First and foremost, go to the Lord in prayer. Ask Him to clarify your need to ask for someone's forgiveness, and then ask Him to begin to prepare the person's heart to receive your request.

Ask God for His forgiveness for offending that person and then for His guidance in how best to proceed. Seeking someone's forgiveness is much too important to just plow ahead. Wait for God's timing. A pastor we once knew said that whenever he had lagged behind in any endeavor, as long as he was seeking God, the Lord had always made up the difference in time. He will do that for you and me as well.

While you're waiting on God, continue in prayer as you determine how best to seek forgiveness. Will you verbalize your request in person or by phone, or will you write it in a note or letter? Both are viable, but here's why I suggest the latter. Receiving a written request gives the other person time to consider your appeal and thoughtfully prepare a response.

Now, I could not suggest to readers to seek forgiveness when necessary without doing it myself. So I prayerfully prepared a letter. Once I slept on my words and made a few alterations the next morning, I gave a copy to my husband and then emailed it to my loved ones (who call me Mamie). Here's what I wrote:

Dear _____

As I'm completing the book on the power of spoken words and their effects on others, I've come to a place where I need to do what I'm suggesting readers do, and that is to ask forgiveness for words I have spoken that may have harmed those I love.

A major theme throughout this book is forgiveness, forgiving others for words spoken to us as well as seeking forgiveness for words we have spoken to others. Forgiveness is not necessarily easy, no matter what side of the words we are on, but it's necessary in order to have healthy relationships with those closest to us.

There are a lot of reasons we say what we say. Sometimes it's out of misunderstanding, hurt, anger, and many other emotions. Sometimes it's just carelessness and not thinking ahead on how our words might damage someone.

Many words have left indelible marks on me, affecting what I say and do, and thankfully I have come to terms with most of them as I've asked the Lord to bring me understanding and then help me forgive and move on.

I too have said words that are sure to have left lasting negative effects on others. No matter what the reason behind them, they should never have been said. And that is why I'm writing to you today.

If I have said words, many years ago or just the other day, that have left you feeling like anything other than the magnificent creation you are, I ask for your forgiveness. You have been placed in my life as a gift from our heavenly Father. I am sorry if I've ever misused or tarnished that gift with negative, careless, or hurtful words.

It may be that we will need to talk so that I can take responsibility for my words and then say I'm sorry more directly. It may be that this form of communication is enough to help clear the air. Only you can decide that.

Please know that I love you and appreciate that our God saw fit to place you in my life. Of all the treasures we can have on earth, nothing is more important than the treasure of family.

I pray you will honestly and thoughtfully consider my request. And please let me know if we should talk.

Mamie

Since I work with words, writing out my thoughts comes a little easier than for most. That may not be the case for you. Feel free to use my words as a springboard if you choose to use this form of seeking forgiveness. If you know your offense, state it specifically. If you don't, you can assume that at some time or another something you said has offended someone. In that case, like mine, your letter can be more general.

There are several online sources with "I'm sorry" messages written out. I don't suggest using them or my letter verbatim, but both might be beneficial as starting points. In any event, prayerfully construct your note or letter, and then send it with the assurance that you've taken a gigantic step in bringing reconciliation and healing to that special relationship.

You're Forgiven, Now What?

Once someone has extended their forgiveness, the relationship may be quite positive, and things are back to normal. On the other hand, someone might offer their forgiveness but still appear a little standoffish.

I live in Florida, a state where it is not unusual to have sinkholes. I didn't think much about it when Bob and I contemplated our move from Michigan, where springtime potholes abound. I did consider, however, there would be alligators, a few more snakes, and bugs—big bugs. I have observed all three since moving here.

As for sinkholes, several, some quite large, have opened up in the two years we've lived in the Sunshine State. Thankfully, none too close to our home. There was, however, a pothole on a street we drive on nearly every day. The hole measured about eighteen inches in diameter. It seemed as though it was there for weeks. No problem, we all just drove around it.

Then one day I noticed the hole had been filled and covered over with asphalt. Interestingly, it was several days before I could drive over the now-covered hole. Not only was I adhering to my new normal for driving around the hole, but I was also just a little leery about driving over it, covered or not. Was it solid and safe?

I wanted evidence. I wanted to give it some time to see if it was really repaired. Yes, I could see the hole was covered.

Yes, I watched others drive right over the asphalt. But for me, I needed to give it some time to trust that the spot would not tear up my tire or, worse, turn into a full-fledged sinkhole and gobble up my car—and me—completely.

That's how it can be when we offer forgiveness to someone. In offering forgiveness or letting go of a debt we feel is owed us, it's easy to continue to operate as before. Just like I continued to go around the hole in the road, we can go around a person, so to speak. We skirt the issue because we're just not sure the same things won't happen again. In other words, we need to see evidence the hole is repaired. Sometimes that takes time.

And so it is when we seek someone's forgiveness. Yes, we are sorry; yes, we try to make amends; yes, we say we will never do or say the same thing again. And though the other person has offered to forgive us, it might take time for them to relax and feel comfortable again in the relationship.

Can holes reoccur? Of course. Can we and others revert to old ways if we are not careful? Sure. If that happens, I hope we can plug up the hole, or fix the relationship breach, sooner rather than later. Old habits die hard. But they can be put to death with commitment, perseverance, and determination to seek out the Lord for direction and to do the right thing for the betterment of those we love and, in the long run, for ourselves.

I now drive comfortably over the area that was once a pothole. It's proven itself, and so I trust it fully. That's how it can be in our relationships too.

Now, what if we've gone humbly to someone, seeking forgiveness, but they refuse? That could be a problem. When it seems like the more we say, the more distance is created, we might offer something like, "I'm sorry you see it that way, and I understand it might take you some time to forgive me. I hope in the future you'll feel differently." Then we release the situation to the Lord and let Him handle it, knowing we've done our part to make amends.

"I Just Can't Forgive Myself"

Have you ever spoken the words "I just can't forgive myself"? I have. But is the need to forgive ourselves necessary or even scriptural?

Perhaps our greatest model for living a Christlike life is the apostle Paul, who did not seem to see the need to forgive himself. At least that's what I'm surmising when I read his words in 1 Corinthians 4:3–4: "I do not even examine myself. For I am conscious of nothing against myself, yet I am not by this acquitted; but the one who examines me is the Lord" (NASB). He is saying that the One who has acquitted him is the Lord, and He's the One who examines Paul. And if he, Paul, has been examined by the Lord and then acquitted, what further need is there for him, Paul, to put himself on trial again?

Yet, we do it all the time. We take what the Lord has forgiven and use it to put ourselves back on the stand, even though we are told in Psalm 103:11–12:

> For as high as the heavens are above the earth,
> So great is His lovingkindness toward those who
> fear Him.
> As far as the east is from the west,
> So far has He removed our transgressions from us.
> (NASB)

You can't get any farther than the east from the west. Saying that even though others have forgiven us and the Lord has forgiven us, we still need to forgive ourselves puts us in a position that says God, the supreme maker and Creator of this universe, the One who knit us together in our mothers' wombs, the omnipotent, omniscient, omnipresent God's forgiveness is not enough for us to move on in life. And so we don't. We revert to our fallen state and to our victim roles. Yes, we have taken the step toward salvation and we've made our reservation for heaven, but life on earth is not all that appealing, thank you very much. And the words we sing are still "Woe is me."

Listen, if God's forgiveness is not enough, then no one else's forgiveness is going to be either—least of which, yours or mine!

The apostle Paul (formerly Saul) had every right to stand back, look inward, and feel the need to forgive himself for the crimes he perpetrated against Christians. But God got ahold of Saul on the road to Damascus (Acts 9) and issued the soon-to-be convert a new assignment—and a new name. Paul took time to grasp his new identity in the Lord, and then he plunged full speed ahead into his new role as apostle, a servant of Christ, and a steward of the mysteries of his God (1 Cor. 4:1).

In Philippians 3:12–14, Paul writes:

> Not that I have already obtained it or have already become perfect, but I press on so that I may lay hold of that for which also I was laid hold of by Christ Jesus. Brethren, I do not regard myself as having laid hold of it yet; but one thing I do: forgetting what lies behind and reaching forward to

what lies ahead, I press on toward the goal for the prize of the upward call of God in Christ Jesus. (NASB)

The key word in this passage is *forgetting*. Paul said that he was making a choice to forget what was behind him. He chose to reach forward to what was ahead, pressing on toward the goal for the prize of the upward call of God in Christ Jesus!

The apostle Paul did not have time to look back and possibly get stuck in his past. Instead of ruminating over what he did or didn't do, he made a deliberate choice to go on and press forward.

I maintain that if the apostle Paul did not have to forgive himself, then neither do we.

But I can hear some of you say, "I just can't get over what I did all those years ago" or just yesterday. Not only do I hear you, I understand. There are so many things I wish I had not done and many others I wish I had. When thoughts arise, often out of the blue, or when a sound or smell or something I see takes me back to my former days, I struggle too.

I brawl with myself often when episodes from my past come back to haunt me. But I have a choice. I can continue the struggle, or I can put those times where they belong—at the feet of Christ, whose shed blood covers every sin I've committed and ever will. Period. And then I need to press on to that high calling of my Savior and Lord. There's nothing in Scripture that says I must forgive myself.

Matt Slick, of the Christian Apologetics and Research Ministry, writes:

> The idea of forgiving yourself carries with it the implication of guilt and the need to be released. . . . Our forgiveness

comes from God because ultimately it is God against whom we have sinned. If you are carrying guilt because of sin and you can't seem to get rid of it, then you need to realize that there is no sin you have committed that cannot be cleansed by the loving sacrifice of Christ. It is not an issue of you forgiving yourself. The issue is whether or not God forgives you. So, go to the cross and know that Jesus has already forgiven you, loves you, and will receive you to Himself.[2]

Eliminating the Need to Seek Forgiveness

How do we guard ourselves from getting into positions where we need to ask for forgiveness, at least in the area of our words?

One way is to practice restraint. I say practice because restraint doesn't come naturally for most of us. We are in too much of a hurry most days and merely blurt out what we are thinking or feeling. We generally don't take time to consider what effects our words could have on someone.

The same is true if there's a lull in our conversation with someone. Why do we feel the need to fill every moment with sound? Less is often better, especially when it comes to words. Once words are spoken, they can never be retrieved. I would much rather *not* say something that I wish I could get back than wish I *had* said something but didn't. I can always offer my thoughtful words later, but I can never retrieve ill-spoken or inconsiderate words.

Another way we can guard ourselves from having to seek forgiveness is to be careful of our tone of voice. After many years of living in several locales, Bob and I landed in Lebanon, Ohio, a mere seven minutes from my daughter Laura's home, where she and her husband resided with four of our grandchildren. I loved it there. Besides family, I had new friends and several writer-clients from the Cincinnati area. It felt like the perfect move.

But Mom, back home in Michigan, began having memory issues and mishaps with her checking account. After much consideration and prayer, Bob and I decided to return to Michigan rather than move Mom out of her apartment of thirty-six years.

One day when Mom and I were in the car, she related a familiar story to me. In just a couple of minutes, she repeated her story. I said something like, "Yeah, Mom, that's what you said." When she told me her story for the third time, using practically the exact words, my response was far from fitting. I said, "Mo-om, you just told me that." Now, mind you, I didn't say those words loudly, but did you notice the emphasis on *Mo-om*? Does that give you an idea of the tone of voice I used, that condescending, belittling, demeaning tone?

Honestly, I was frustrated, tired of living on an emotional roller coaster, and just a little put out that we gave up our home in Ohio. And it showed in my voice—to my precious mother. I can remember her forlorn look. She had to be wondering why her daughter was talking to her like that.

I went to bed that night, crying out to the Lord to give me more patience in dealing with the invisible monster called dementia. It wasn't Mom's fault and certainly not of her choosing to end up with this ugly disease.

There is something positive about dementia though. Mom soon forgot our conversation. But I haven't, and I'm not sure I ever will. I have repented of that day and I know God has forgiven me, but I still feel remorse when I share this story.

From that point on, I have tried to watch my tone of voice. Sometimes it's not the words we speak but rather the way we speak them. And it's usually to the ones closest to us. I would never speak to a friend, or even a stranger, in the tone of voice I used with Mom that day.

True Restoration

I'm ending this chapter with an example I believe amplifies what it means to ask for someone's forgiveness. Dr. Shann Ferch shares about the first time he saw "asking for forgiveness in action." It all began when he observed his future father-in-law make a sharp comment at the dinner table to his future mother-in-law.

After dinner, Dr. Ferch said his father-in-law came over and asked for his forgiveness for how he treated his wife at dinner. "You don't have to ask me," Dr. Ferch said.

His father-in-law replied, "No, I don't ask just for you. In our family, we ask forgiveness of the person whom we harmed, and everybody who was there, in order to restore the dignity of the one who was harmed."[3]

Truly, this father-in-law, while he may have been a little reckless with his words toward his wife at dinner, understands the need for dignity and someone's self-esteem, something we are going to talk about more in chapter 12.

it's **your** turn

1. Is there someone whose forgiveness you need to seek? If so, what might be your best approach?

2. What steps might you take to ensure your words to others do not convey condemnation?

3. If you've asked for someone's forgiveness, what has been their reaction?

4. Do you, like many of us, tend to carry around regret? After reading this chapter, how might you feel better equipped to deal with remorse?

12

letting go

> To be misunderstood even by those whom one loves is the cross and bitterness of life. It is the secret of that sad melancholy smile on the lips of great men which so few understand. It is what must have oftenest wrung the heart of the Son of Man.
>
> HENRI-FREDERIC AMIEL

Words reverberated in his head. Although they were uttered decades before, they stuck with him still. "Why would you want to do that?" his father queried most often when young Jack told him about something he thought of doing. From the smallest of actions to more major attempts, the first words out of his father's mouth echoed the same sentiment. And most often, his young son heard disdain instead of encouragement or the approval he so desired from his father.

Important to young Jack, even as he advanced in years, was to hear his father say something positive about what he was doing. So Jack, in his striving, tried one thing after the other, seeking that one endeavor that might gain him affirmative recognition. This became a pattern. Starting something, but not following through—whether in business, relationships, or home projects—led to brokenness and what could be perceived as failures, the exact opposite of what Jack was after.

The title of this chapter is "Letting Go." Interestingly, however, is that even if Jack's father could have, at some point in his son's formative years, prepared him for responsible and accomplished manhood, his words were not "letting go." They were etched in Jack's subconscious to haunt him for years to come.

Perhaps Jack's dad echoed what he heard growing up. Maybe his own parents could not understand the dreams and desires of their son and so did not give him the encouragement he may have sought. Perhaps he himself did not reach out to disturb the status quo, and so he expected his son to follow the party line: to farm, to work for the family business, or to get an eight-to-five job in the local factory. In the eyes of his family, those ambitions would have proven him to be a responsible young man. But Jack had other desires. And Jack never did hear his father say, "Good job, Son!"

Before we are tempted to misunderstand and judge Jack for his desire for approval or to judge his father, for that matter, it would be wise to realize, even admit, that Jack's yearning was not unusual. It's common among many if not all of us to want to please our parents.

If you have children, then surely you've heard them call out as they try something new, "Look at me, Mom!" "Watch me, Dad!" It starts early, because innately we all have the need for significance. We all want to feel valued, esteemed, admired, and worthy. Down deep, we all hunger to hear words of affirmation. In fact, to flourish, we need to hear a lot of attaboys and attagirls. That's just the way we're wired.

There are other basic needs we all have, which Dr. Abraham Maslow delineated for study back in the 1940s when he developed his Hierarchy of Needs. If you've taken a college course in human psychology, you were probably introduced to his theory.

Briefly, Dr. Maslow believed every person is born with certain basic needs. And to successfully progress in life, it is paramount these needs are met. His original study came out as a five-layer pyramid with the most basic of requirements—food, water, sleep, and shelter—being the foundation. Going up the pyramid from there, the levels were safety and security, social, self-esteem, and self-actualization.

Dr. Maslow theorized that until man's most basic needs are met, none of the other levels will matter; he saw the needs as progressional. In later years, he rearranged the levels somewhat to add the need for knowledge, the need for aesthetics, and the need for transcendence, making it eight levels of basic needs we all have.[1]

Now let's observe what God's Word says about each of these needs. In the physiological area of *food*, *water*, and *sleep*, all four Gospels tell the story of Jesus feeding the 5,000. In John 4:1–14, we read about Jesus offering water to a Samaritan woman. In the area of sleep, perhaps the most well-known verse is Matthew 11:28: "Come to me, all you who are weary and burdened, and I will give you rest."

The phrase "fear not" appears 365 times in the Bible, so it's clear God is concerned about our *safety* and *security*.

Since we are wired for connectivity and relationships, concerning our *social needs*, God tells us not to forsake the gathering of believers. In addition, He often talks of friends and brothers and sisters in the faith—the brethren.

"Love your neighbor as yourself" is the second greatest commandment (Mark 12:31). Clearly, to love our neighbor properly, we need to know how to *esteem* ourselves, the creations God made us to be.

In Jeremiah 29:11, He tells us He knows the plans He has for us. That says to me He is concerned about our *self-actualization*.

The entire book of Proverbs addresses getting and using *knowledge*.

In the area of *aesthetics*, we read in Genesis that when God created the world, He looked around at all He had made and said it was good (Gen. 1:31).

If there's any question about our innate need to go beyond ourselves—*transcendence*—just recall the help given by service groups and individual volunteers who traveled miles to reach out to thousands upon thousands in the aftermath of Hurricanes Harvey and Irma and in so many other disasters in our nation. It's happening as I write this chapter. Rescue crews are still active in Houston, while many other teams are at the ready to travel throughout the state of Florida. Yes, for many it's their job, but that's not the case for everyone. Countless others have chosen to go outside themselves, leaving homes and loved ones to reach out to others. Here we have Scripture's Golden Rule in action, doing for others as we would like others to do for us (Matt. 7:12).

Dr. Maslow brought these basic needs to light in the modern age, but it's clear God had them in mind long before the good doctor entered the world. And since there is nothing new under the sun (Eccles. 1:9), I assert that Dr. Maslow merely paraphrased what God wrote in His Word about the basic needs of the human beings He created.

So then, these are common needs of us all. They are beautiful and reasonable needs. You see, it was only normal that young Jack—and later mature Jack—sensed this need for significance. He so desperately wanted to hear words that affirmed his worth. When he didn't hear them at an early age, he carried around a motto that said he didn't meet certain standards, which, in turn, caused him to strive for the approval he was never going to get. That does not make for happy and satisfied living.

Believe it or not, how our basic needs are met—or not met—will contribute to the words we speak and how we respond to words spoken to us. Think about it. If I'm hungry, tired, or not feeling safe, I'm probably not going to be all that receptive to someone's words. If I'm the one speaking, I may come across as being abrupt, inconsiderate, and maybe even mean-spirited. I'm not going to list each of the eight basic needs and how I might be affected by the words of others or how my words could leave my less-than-happy mouth if those needs aren't being met. You can draw those conclusions for yourself.

What's important to remember is the next time you are tempted to talk with someone who is hungry, tired, fearful, feeling a lack of self-esteem, and so on, consider how your words might magnify their discomfort or how your words could alleviate and fulfill some of what they might be lacking, especially in the area of self-esteem. Sometimes someone just needs to feel valued. With your tongue, you have the power to make them feel more threatened or more at ease.

Stop, Look, and Listen

Today I did something simple to let my husband know he is important to me and that what he has to say matters. In the middle of writing this chapter, I heard the door to our outdoor area—where I was writing—open and then quickly close. Bob had been out running errands. When he opened the door to say hello and saw that I was working, he went back inside so as not to disturb me. I appreciated his thoughtfulness, but since I was ready for a break, I invited him to come and sit with me.

As soon as he did, I saved this file, closed my laptop, and gave him my full attention. In other words, I stopped, I looked at him, and I listened to what he had to say. In that brief encounter, I helped to meet some of his basic needs: safety, social, and self-esteem.

Am I always that attentive? Like the rest of us, I get caught up in my work, social media, and whatever else occupies my time, but I'm getting better. Just working on this project has heightened my sensitivity to the importance of taking time to show those I love they are important to me and I appreciate who they are.

Not-So-Healthy Needs

Just as there are healthy and reasonable needs all humans have, there are some that aren't so healthy. In fact, they have been known to get in the way of our succeeding and living full and meaningful lives. Before we look at a few of the not-so-healthy needs, let's look at the word *strive*.

Recall a few paragraphs earlier where we talked about Jack not being satisfied as a child and young man. His endeavors to get parental approval became a type of striving. To *strive* means to "make great efforts to achieve or obtain something; to struggle or fight vigorously for something." Synonyms for *strive* are "try hard, endeavor, exert oneself, do one's best." I think we get the picture.

Now, when someone has done the best they can and still is not receiving the recognition they desperately desire, unhealthy needs can present themselves—needs that can take the life right out of a person, such as having to be in control or having to be right or having to please. Striving can lead to stress, disappointment, lack of fulfillment, feelings of failure, and so much more. Let's take a closer look at some of these not-so-healthy needs.

The Need to Please

When I received my latest edition of *The Writer* magazine, I was impressed with the lead story by Ekta R. Garg. The author had experienced early on words from her father that she said left her "confidence bleeding."[2]

Sometime during her high school years, Ekta's father asked her what she wanted to do with her life. She told him she wanted to be a writer. He responded, "Writers are a dime a dozen." Believing her parents would support her in whatever she chose to do, she said she remembered nothing else from that conversation.

And so it is with many of us who dream just a little outside the box of a normal nine-to-five job with benefits and regularity. Often, others look at the practical while we look at the ideal. In the process, our hopes and dreams get dashed by the people we hope will be on our sides, even our cheerleaders.

Ekta admitted she didn't see the practical side of her dad's concern at that time. Naturally, he wanted his daughter to live a financially secure life. He loved his daughter and wanted the best for her.

Eventually, those closest to Ekta would appreciate her writing and the course her life was taking. But all she seemed to feel from her parents, even her husband, who was most supportive of her career, was an almost who-cares attitude.

Have you ever felt that way in your chosen line of work? Or maybe it's a ministry you want to support or even lead. Maybe it's a study group you'd like to begin around a topic you are passionate about. Maybe it's your decision to be a stay-at-home parent and homeschool your children. Who really cares, anyway?

In an online course Ekta took to learn how to navigate the literary magazine world, her instructor assigned the class to cut out a one-inch-square piece of paper and write on it the names of all those whose opinions on their writing they valued. If students couldn't fit all the names on that one-inch square, they were to edit their list.

You can imagine the angst one might feel to have a one-inch-square piece of paper to write anything on, much less a list. In tiny letters, Ekta wrote down two names and then added "me."

The point is when you try to please a multitude of people or work hard to get their approval, you are going to be disappointed—for a lot of reasons. First, no one totally understands your heart, so what is vastly important to you will not always be to them. Second, generally, everyone else is trying to please and get the approval of others themselves and are probably not really concerned with your dreams. And third, too often, pleasing someone else or getting their approval is based on feelings, and we know how dangerous that can be as feelings can change momentarily.

Consider taking a piece of writing paper and making a list of those people whose approval you'd like to obtain, either generally or in a special endeavor. Start with your Creator and end with yourself. In between might be those in your closest circle of influence, those with whom you do life. But keep in mind they too have dreams, desires, and issues.

I trust you are blessed like Ekta, who had two writer friends she could rely on for love and complete support. About her writing, she says that if anyone's opinion matters, it's most certainly hers.

While I desire respect and admiration from everyone I meet, the opinions that matter most to me are my husband's and those of my immediate family members—that is, after God's, of course. If I truly believe I am pleasing Him, then I can only hope those closest to me are pleased too.

The Need to Be Right

I would not perceive myself as one needing to be right all the time. In fact, at times I've had information to add about something being discussed but didn't say anything. I'm working on when to speak up and when not to. It serves me well. When I haven't heeded my own advice, I have suffered the consequences, immediately knowing when I've said too much. But I've found that some needs, like that of having to be right, come disguised.

How is this need masked? Do you ever correct other people when what they are saying is wrong—at least, wrong in your eyes? Maybe it's wrong facts or details about a topic you know something about. When my husband is relating a story, my biggest tendency is to interject what I think is the correct information. I'm learning, however, that often it's just a difference in perception—his versus mine. He relates something as he sees or has seen it. I interrupt and jump in to set the record straight, when really my words are just how I perceived that same event. I'm not alone in this. I see it regularly when in the company of other couples.

Another way this need is masked is by redoing what someone else has done. In one of my retail detours several years ago, I worked in linens at a major department store. My new manager showed me how to fold and shelve towels; I fold them the same way today. Bob, however, does not. And since he doesn't, I've been known to take them apart and refold them.

It hit me one day that my actions were saying to Bob in no uncertain terms that he needed correction. Instead of appreciating my husband's act of service, I chose to make sure the towels were folded right. Come to find out, Bob folds towels the way he was taught for military inspection.

Young moms do the same thing to young dads. Is that why a lot of new fathers stay clear of their new babies—for fear of not doing something right? Parents do it to children when they redo something the child has done. And the list could be expanded.

Keep in mind, not only does our redoing someone's work or correcting details in their stories make us look superior in our own minds, but our actions also imply to those we love "I'm right and you're wrong" or "You can't do anything right."

Remember, our brains are wired to slant to the negative. No matter how many times I thank my husband for doing the dishes or washing the laundry or taking such good care of our yard, what most likely will leave a lasting impression is when I correct him or redo something he's done.

Now really, does it matter how towels are folded? Will my houseguests care? Does it matter if I think some details of a story aren't right? Will the listener even know the difference? Is it worth harming my special relationships—or worse, giving those I love the impression they just don't measure up?

Another example of someone having the need to be right came to me at a recent writers' conference I attended. At lunch one afternoon, a new friend, whom I'll call Michelle, and I talked almost from the moment we began our meal until we finished. One talking point led to another, and soon I was telling her about the book I was writing on the power of spoken words.

After giving her a few examples, Michelle shared from her own arsenal of stories. The most poignant was about her husband who was an attorney, a brilliant man and strong in his opinions. He never hesitated to argue his case, even in their marital affairs. She said for many years she never won an argument with him and finally grew tired of all their "discussions" ending in his favor, even when she knew her points were valid. Now, this was a good marriage, a great marriage, in fact, except for this one area.

One day it struck her that the chances of her ever winning an argument with her husband were little to none. After all, he was a lawyer, trained (and paid) to win his cases, and no doubt with a gift for doing so. She came up with a plan.

The next time they got into a discussion that needed to go one way or the other, once her husband made his case, she said something like, "I hear what you're saying, and I'd like some time to think about it. I'll get back with you." Sometimes she got back with him; often, she did not. Either way, she no longer felt outnumbered, outwitted, outmaneuvered, and, most of all, powerless. In fact, she felt the opposite. She was now in a position of power over the words meant to outsmart her. Yes, my new friend had made a deliberate choice to no longer be the victim.

Do you find yourself in a marriage—or any situation, for that matter—such as Michelle's, where no matter what you say, you feel as though you always come out on the losing end? It might be with a spouse, a parent, an employer, even a friend. If so, do you think you could use Michelle's words the next time you find yourself in that position? You might want to practice saying them out loud: "I hear what you're saying, and I'd like some time to think about it. I'll get back with you."

Another topic Michelle and I discussed was choosing our battles. Some discussions absolutely need to take place. Many do not. So besides encouraging herself by using the words above, Michelle has also learned what issues are worth going to the mat for. Another great lesson from my new friend.

The Need to Be in Control

Similar to the need to be right is the need to be in control. The older I get, the more I realize I'm in control of very little.

Even when I think I have the perfect plan for something I want to do or see happen, I'm reminded of the Scripture verse that tells us people make their plans, but the Lord directs their steps (Prov. 16:9). Not that God is a big interferer with what His kids want to do, but rather He sees the beginning from the end and has our best interest in mind. If my plans aren't going to benefit me, often my heavenly Father intervenes and works things out for my good. It may not appear that way at first, but down the road, looking back, I have thanked Him over and over for not allowing those plans to come to fruition.

As parents, we want to be in control of our children, which is understandable. Like our heavenly Father, we want what's best for them. If they are making decisions detrimental to their well-being, we want to take control—and should. And that's a good thing, when our children are young and under our care and need our protection, our boundaries, and our full attention.

As they become adults, however, it's a much different matter. They now have the right to make their own choices, even if their choices are harmful. At that point, we may have opportunities for input, but we no longer have control. Yet, it's hard letting go, isn't it?

It's hard to sit back and watch those we love make unwise choices. We want to go in and rescue our adult children, fix their problems, protect and, yes, *control* them. Too often, what happens is a natural pushback, and in too many instances a relationship breach occurs. And now if we parents do have sound advice to offer, their ears are closed. So much could be written here, but I will refrain except to say that once our children are adults, I believe we owe them the same respect we desire from them.

Instead of circumstances, let's be in control of our choices. Instead of others, let's be in control of our own words and actions.

The Need to Know

I've come to believe that some things are not for us to know. Some things are detrimental for us to know. Some things are so far out of our control that our knowing all the details makes little difference in their outcomes but all the difference in our mental and emotional states.

Recall my needing to know how Northern California was faring during the massive fires in October 2017. For many reasons, I have an emotional tie to that place and its people, so I sat glued to my computer for several days on end. One week turned into two and the fires were still not contained. What of our friends? What of the beautiful mountains and vineyards and monuments? I needed to know. How did it start? How was it being fought? What about the thousands of evacuees? I needed to know.

Here's the result of my needing to know. I became depressed. I lost out on a great amount of writing time. I became introspective and just wanted to be alone. And do you know, the fires continued to rage, the fires continued to be fought, and the evacuees continued to be evacuated. Absolutely nothing changed for the better as a result of my needing to know. There was not one thing I could do to change the situation.

As I worked on this chapter, fires raged in another part of California, this time in and around Ventura County, another place I've lived that I thought was heaven on earth. Honestly, once again, I was tempted to keep going back to Facebook and news channels and other online information centers. I wanted to know so badly the whys and what fors.

I could keep checking and grow ever more saddened by this turn of events, or I could keep my nose to the proverbial grindstone and complete my writing while continuing to offer up my prayers for the place and its people. My knowing blow-by-blow what was transpiring on the opposite side of the country would change nothing.

So instead, I chose to focus on my work and on what I knew for sure—that the God of the universe, the One who created me and who sustains me, knows and loves me beyond comprehension.

Recently, I followed Facebook postings of a new grandmother. The joy and absolute adoration she had at the birth of her first grandchild went beyond what words could describe. She posted, "I'm in love!," "I'm smitten," "I can't get enough of him," "I don't know if I can stand not seeing him for two days," and her posts went on. I understand. I have experienced new grandchildren eleven times. There are no words that adequately express the love a grandmother has for each baby. Multiply that times infinity and you have the love our Father in heaven has for each one of us, whether we reciprocate His love or not. And that's really all we need to know for sure.

The Need for More

It seems we live in an era where more is equated with better. More technology, more money, more things, more status, more, more, more.

We want better ways of doing things, and rightfully so. I'm grateful for our modern technology, especially after losing a lot of it during Hurricane Irma due to downed power lines.

There's nothing wrong with the concept of more as long as we don't turn into striving machines for more, bigger, and better, all the while overlooking the here and now and what we have at our fingertips.

Hurricanes are not fun to experience. Thankfully, our area of Florida did not get the high winds and water that many other parts of the state received. Although parts of our county were hit quite hard, our immediate community was only without power for about fourteen hours. Others in the state, during a period of extremely hot weather, were without power for days on end.

I can say for myself, and I'm sure I can testify for others, the time we spent without electricity, and many without an adequate water supply, caused us to truly appreciate what we did have and then what was returned to us once power was restored. Disasters do that to people. We learn to appreciate the little things in life.

American author Napoleon Hill, known best for his book *Think and Grow Rich*, stated: "Your big opportunity may be right where you are now."[3]

I'm grateful to be able to say that if nothing else ever comes my way, I have life here and now and a promise of life in the hereafter with my Savior. I live in a country that still allows me the protection of life, liberty, and the pursuit of happiness. I have a loving husband and wonderful children and grandchildren. I have a church body that's my extended family. I have friends. I have good health and my basic needs are met. And I have work I love. What *more* is there that would fulfill me or make me any happier than I am right now?

Don't miss out on what you have right at your fingertips: your life, your health, your family, your home, your employment, your friends. If you're in search of something more and better, keep in mind, your more and better just might be where you are right now and what you have in hand this very moment.

it's **your** turn

1. In your inventory of the eight basic human needs, how would you rate yourself in each area? List ways to improve those levels in which you rate low.

2. Describe a time when you stopped what you were doing and gave your full attention to another person. How did it seem to make them feel? How did it make you feel?

3. We listed five areas of unhealthy needs. How would you rate yourself in each of those areas?

4. Right here, right now, write out what you have to be grateful for, and keep your list handy for ready reference.

13

free at last

The fear of man strangles us, because we can never please everybody; but the fear of the Lord frees us, because it challenges us to live and serve for an audience of One.

PAUL CHAPPELL

ree at last, free at last. Thank God Almighty, we are free at last." Dr. Martin Luther King Jr. made these words popular when he closed his famous "I Have a Dream" speech during the March on Washington for Jobs and Freedom on August 28, 1963. Those words were made synonymous with the American dream of Dr. King and many others, both historical and contemporary, desiring to see all peoples of this nation—and around the world—walk freely in their God-given rights of equality, opportunity, and safety.

In addition to the rights listed above, I'd like to think that we who have been harmed by the negligent and careless words of others will finally walk totally free of the effects of those words. Dr. King borrowed from an old Negro spiritualist whose hymn reflected that the writer knew *total* freedom would come when, in the air, he would meet his Savior face-to-face.

And so it will be for us who have chosen to believe in the Good News of Jesus Christ. Our total freedom from harmful and damaging words will come then, for sure. In the meantime though, how can we live as free as possible in the here and now? How can we face each new day with a newfound freedom that suggests the only words we're going to take to heart are those that reflect the words in God's love letter to His people?

How to Be Free at Last

I offer seven steps to consider on your way to total freedom from hurting words.

Step 1: Remember Who and Whose You Are

Paramount to keep in mind is that you are *not* the negative words implied by others' spoken words. You are God's image bearer, knit together by design. You have a future and a hope, and you can have the assurance of living eternally with Him in heaven.

So, know your gifts and strengths, and then act on your personal and special DNA—for your satisfaction in life and for God's glory.

As you walk in your unique gifts and strengths, stay true to your calling. Just as your Creator knit you together with a special pattern that's only yours, He has a purpose for you, one that others may not totally understand or want to support. Rest assured, however, you were created with a reason to be, and with that reason to be comes all the tools necessary for you to carry out your destiny here on earth.

The moment you were born, you arrived fully furnished to live out the life God has for you. As you grow and progress through life, knowledge will be revealed and equipping will be provided at just the right time.

Jim Elliot was the husband of writer and speaker Elisabeth Elliot and one of five fellow missionaries murdered by the Auca Indians in 1956. Elisabeth writes in her book *Shadow of the Almighty* that her husband knew what it meant to live free in Christ. He knew the importance of seeking only the approval of his almighty God and not that of people. Before he went to the jungles of South America, many misunderstood his calling and therefore spoke negatively into his dream. But Jim said:

> To me the words and worries of the rest matter not at all. It has been a long lesson learning to live only before God and letting Him teach the conscience and to fear nothing save missing His will. But we are learning, and I would live no other way. I want always to say with the Apostle, "God is my judge."[1]

Oh, how many more of us could experience joy instead of constantly looking over our shoulders to see who is watching and who might be judging our actions? God's Word says that when Jesus sets us free, we are free indeed (John 8:36). We do not need to be bothered by what others think, especially if their call is different from ours or if they choose not to try to understand what calls our heart.

To Jim Elliot, missionary work to the Indians of Ecuador called his heart and the hearts of the other men in his party who took the gospel to the Amazon. What's calling your heart? Will others understand? Perhaps not; sometimes we don't understand ourselves. Others did not appreciate Jim Elliot's call, but he forged ahead anyway. We need to consider doing the same. That tug, that yearning you feel, is an indicator of God's purpose for you. Jim Elliot and the other four men knew their purpose. You and I can know ours too.

Despite the words of others, Jim pursued his call. Bob and I did something similar when we too followed an uncommon call. It began shortly after we married in 1993. It was a journey not many, if any, in our family or circle of friends understood. Some scoffed at our intention. In fact, we didn't understand it either, it was so unusual. Had I been on the other end of the situation, I too might have questioned, even criticized, our decision. I should say decisions, for we made similar choices many times in the first several years of our lives together as our journey continued.

The short story is we married in January and by May had put all our belongings—except our computers, toiletries, some clothes, a few kitchen items, and books—into storage and bought a twenty-four-foot travel trailer and a pickup truck to pull it.

We left Michigan with an itinerary to stop off at friends in Pittsburgh before visiting editors, churches, and Christian events, including a Bible conference in Tulsa and Promise Keepers in Boulder, Colorado. From there, we had plans to stop off in Northern California to meet up with family and then journey to Southern California, where our planned itinerary stopped. We believed the Lord would give us instructions once there. So when we said our goodbyes in Michigan on that bright day in May of 1993, we had no idea when and if we would return.

There is so much more I could tell you about our journey, but the point I want to make is that we did something quite out of the ordinary, and our actions were not always understood, welcomed, or appreciated. Yet, both Bob and I were always in agreement and in prayer, asking for signs and clear direction from the Lord. Did we get it all right? I'm sure we missed a few signals. But as best as we could decipher, we did what we felt God had called us to do. We gave up most of what we owned but received something so much greater: new experiences, new friends, and a closer walk with the Lord as we watched Him at work in the lives of hundreds around the country.

We went against convention and the doubts, criticisms, and ill wishes of others for something far better in return. You may have to do that too to stay free. Others might not understand and may say things that hurt deeply. Remember, it's not about you. It's about where they are in life and the condition of their hearts. Often, the ones we leave behind, whether literally or theoretically, feel abandoned, hurt, maybe even envious. From those feelings, hurting words can emanate.

Will we always get it right? Most likely there will be times when we mishear or in haste make choices that aren't perfect for each situation. But be sure that even if we don't quite hit the mark in our timing and decision-making, if our hearts are set on seeking after God, He will always make up the difference. We witnessed that time and time again.

Step 2: Forgive Daily

Daily, we deal with words—our own and those of others. That means that every day we will have opportunities to extend forgiveness. In my research, I came across a plethora of unkind and condescending words spoken to others—from demeaning remarks to threats of murder. While the words each of us has heard are different in scope and intensity, what we all have in common is the need to forgive those who have issued hurtful words, especially if we want to walk in freedom and move on in life.

I liken this to holding the key that will unlock the doors of the prisons some of us find ourselves in. Think of a jailer throwing someone into a prison cell. I'll use myself as an example. Once I'm in the cell, the jailer slams the door shut, turns the key in the lock, and then dangles that key in the air while jeering at me.

But there's good news. The jailer may hold the key to the cell door, but the jailer does not hold the key to my heart, broken as it may be. I, and only I, have the essential key that will unlock the door from the inside. And that key is the willingness to forgive my jailer. You hold that key too. With that key, you can dismiss, release, pardon, set at liberty, deliver, and free the jailer, and in freeing the jailer, you free yourself.

Step 3: Set and Keep Good Boundaries

Now that you've attained a level of freedom, who and what will you allow into your personal space? When we think of boundaries, we often think of fences, which keep both something in and something out. Use the Scriptures as the material for your fences. In other words, stay inside the Word of God and you will be better equipped to make wise choices about every area of your life.

Step 4: Seek Community

Vital to getting and staying free is seeking others to whom we can voice our feelings without returning to the victim mode. Most often, we will find these people in a community of believers. There's good reason God tells us not to forsake gathering together (Heb. 10:25). He knows how important it is for His people to be among others in the faith.

When we are isolated and remain in our own little worlds, we become sullen, we overthink, we overanalyze the words of someone else, and we begin to feel as though no one really understands us or cares. When we make it a point to be with others, we tend to take better care of ourselves, we give and take in conversations and mutual activities, we see the needs of others and others see our needs. I cannot stress enough the importance of getting into community, whether it's gathering regularly with other believers, joining a small group, or meeting around a hobby or special interest.

Step 5: Stop Negativity

Desiree Ayres copastors In His Presence Church in Woodland Hills, California, with her husband, Mel Ayres. Before pastoring, Desiree was a Hollywood stuntwoman. After a failed stunt, Desiree found herself in a burn center in critical condition with second- and third-degree burns and fighting for her life. Ten days later, miraculously healed and whole,

Desiree left the hospital. You can read her story in her book *Beyond the Flame*.

There are many spiritual keys Desiree and her husband used to walk through the entrance of the burn center and only ten days later walk out the exit because of the miracle God performed in her life. At least two of those keys centered around spoken words.

First, Desiree's husband arranged for the Bible to be read aloud or played in her hospital room 24/7. Either people read and declared the Scriptures over Desiree or she would meditate on the recorded versions of His Word to build her faith for healing. They stood on Romans 10:17, which says that faith comes from hearing and hearing by the Word of God.

Second, Desiree closed the door to negativity. A few days into her hospital stay, Desiree had enough strength to move her arms and pick up the phone in her room to answer it. Most of the people in the body of Christ who called or visited did so with words of encouragement. One day, however, she received a call from a friend who said, "Oh, Desiree, you poor thing. I had my back burned once, and it was *soooo* painful. I know what you're going through."[2]

Desiree said she began to feel sorrow, grief, fear, and self-pity. She could have sobbed over the fact that her entire face and other parts of her body were burned and that she felt tremendous pain. But she knew that sympathy and words of sorrow would not help her get her miracle. While her friend meant well, what Desiree needed to hear were words that built her faith, not words of sympathy.

That day, Desiree unplugged her phone and instructed the hospital staff not to let anyone in her room except her husband and her father, her two prayer generals. Desiree made a hard decision that day, but she knew that for her healing she needed to block negative words, even well-meaning words, from her life.

Step 6: Remain Grateful

Like many of us, author Ann Voskamp had her share of heartache. She probably still does, since life can be that way. But Ann discovered early on that when she gave thanks for the life she already had, she found the life she always wanted.

A genius at finding joy in the smallest of things, Ann tells her story in her book *One Thousand Gifts*.[3] Ann writes that she finds joy in such things as boys humming hymns, laughter, the squeak of an old swing swaying. She has learned what many of us need to learn in the hectic, crisis-laden lives we tend to live. When our modern conveniences should allow for more secluded and quiet times, more tender moments with our loved ones, more rest and solace, we have only amped up our speed to do more, accomplish more, excel more, more, more.

Ann's heart was broken at an early age. She lost her beloved little sister to a horrible accident. But Ann was not content to let her broken heart rule her life. She learned along the way that change requires more than merely thinking warm and fuzzy thoughts. Change involves intentionality. She knew she had to do something. And so she began with a dare to herself. And that was the beginning of her gift list—not the gifts she wanted but the gifts she already had.

Her list started out with morning shadows across her old floors, jam piled high on her toast, the cry of a blue jay from high in a spruce tree. The list went on until she reached 1,000, but it didn't stop there. She continually finds gifts for which to be thankful. This is what it means to sing a new song, a song of gratitude and joy, a song that touches not only the singer but those who hear her song. It is encouragement to the soul in its purest form.

Whether you use a calendar or notebook, begin as soon as you're able to make a list of the gifts you already have and the things for which you are grateful. Following Hurricane Irma and the loss of power for several hours while writing this book, I can tell you that just flipping on a light switch gives me much for which to be thankful. Being able to make a cup of coffee rates right up there too. Oh, how spoiled we are in the Western world for sure. Shame on us ever to complain when we have so much for which to be thankful.

Are there times of sadness? Of course. Will there be times of severe crisis? I pray not, but there could be. Is it okay to share our sadness with the Lord and with those who will listen with open hearts, people who will encourage us with their words and not take us further into despair? Of course, it is. That's what living in community is all about.

Is it good to keep singing the same old joyless and ungrateful song? No, no, a thousand times no! It does you and your listener no good at all. It will only serve to bring your soul down more.

Instead, learn to be thankful. I pray that whatever negative circumstance you find yourself in, there will be relief soon. In the midst of what you're going through, however, look for bright spots. Look for ways to encourage yourself with your words of gratefulness and praise to the God who created you and loves you unceasingly.

Step 7: Reach Out to Others

We talked about this earlier, but I don't know of a better way to bring this book to a close than to emphasize how important it is to get outside of ourselves and reach out to others. Even in your dire circumstances? Yes, especially then. And when you do, I believe you will be amazed at how much easier it is to walk—even run—toward the victory God has waiting just for you.

Sometimes my sweetest gratification comes when I've looked a stranger in the eye and with a smile bid them a good day, or complimented someone in the grocery line about an article of their clothing, or used my words to encourage a young mom and dad walking in the mall hand in hand with their little ones. In fact, I make it a practice to get out of myself daily and look for ways to show kindness and respect to others. It costs me nothing but a little bit of time and energy, yet the rewards are priceless.

Freely Walk Out Your Destiny

As a young man, Walt Disney was told, "You don't have any creative, original ideas."

A schoolmaster said of Albert Einstein when Einstein was ten years old, "You will never amount to much."

Ludwig van Beethoven was criticized by a music teacher who said of the now famous musician, "As a composer, he is hopeless."[4]

Thankfully, for reasons most likely known only by them, Disney, Einstein, Beethoven, and many others just like them did not let initial failures and the negative words of others rob them of their destinies. Don't let someone else rob you of your destiny. One day you too will be able to say, "Free at last, free at last!" Until then, walk in the freedom from hurting words God has for you today.

it's **your** turn

1. Name a time when something you felt strongly about was misunderstood. How did you handle it? If it happened again today, would you handle it differently? If so, explain how.

2. On your way to complete freedom from hurting words, is there still a "jailer" you need to forgive? What steps will you take to do so?

3. If you have people in your life who regularly speak negativity into your life, what steps might you take to eliminate their less-than-positive words?

4. Author Ann Voskamp made a list of the gifts she already had. What simple pleasures in your life make up the gifts you already have?

final words

In closing, I leave you with the following poem:

> I shall not pass this way again,
> But far beyond earth's "where and when,"
> May I look back along the road
> Where on both sides good seed I sowed.
>
> I shall not pass this way again;
> May wisdom guide my tongue and pen,
> And love be mine, that so I may
> Plant roses all along the way.
>
> I shall not pass this way again;
> Grant me to soothe the hearts of men,
> Faithful to friends, true to my God;
> A fragrance on the path I trod.
>
> Author Unknown[1]

I'm not going to pass this way again, and neither are you. While we're here, let's choose to speak words that leave a legacy of encouragement, love, and life. And let's walk in the liberty God has for each and every one of us. Truly, there is freedom from hurting words.

notes

Chapter 1 Up Close and Personal

1. *Ragamuffin*, directed by David Leo Shultz (Los Angeles: Color Green Films, 2014), imdb.com/title/tt2412568/plotsummary?ref_=tt_ov_pl.

2. "Lee and Leslie Strobel Discuss *The Case for Christ*" on Pure Talk, YouTube, March 8, 2017, www.bing.com/videos/search?q=pure+talk+lee+strobel&&view=detail&mid=DB030EDDCE6DF2153D26DB030EDDCE6DF2153D26&&FORM=VDRVRV.

3. David A. Seamands, *Putting Away Childish Things* (Wheaton: Victor Books, 1982).

4. Seamands, *Putting Away Childish Things*, 30–31.

5. Mary Kay Ash, *Miracles Happen* (New York: HarperCollins, 1981).

Chapter 2 Seeing the Words for What They Really Are

1. Wendy Walters, Facebook post, April 28, 2015, used by permission.

Chapter 3 Choosing to Forgive

1. Stormie Omartian, *Stormie* (Eugene, OR: Harvest House, 1986), 43.

2. Omartian, *Stormie*, 88.

3. Rudyard Kipling, "I Keep Six Honest Serving Men," Goodreads, accessed August 15, 2018, goodreads.com/quotes/413263-i-keep-six-honest-serving.

4. Laura Hillenbrand, *Unbroken* (New York: Random House, 2010).

5. *Captured by Grace*, directed by Dave Iverson (Charlotte, NC: Billy Graham Evangelistic Association, 2014).

6. *Forgiving Dr. Mengele*, directed by Bob Hercules and Cheri Pugh (Chicago: Media Process Group, 2006).

7. Kitty Chappell, *Soaring Above the Ashes on the Wings of Forgiveness* (Mustang, OK: Tate Publishing, 2013), 64.

8. Chappell, *Soaring Above the Ashes*, 123.

9. Tim Clinton, "Forgiveness," Dr. Tim Clinton, 2001, timclinton.com /articles/30/forgiveness.

10. Cynthia Heald, *Becoming a Woman of Excellence* (Colorado Springs: NavPress, 1986).

Chapter 4 The Truth about You

1. "What It Means to Be 'Made in the Image of God,'" Focus on the Family, August 15, 2018, focusonthefamily.com/family-q-and-a/faith /what-it-means-to-be-made-in-the-image-of-God, emphasis original.

2. Ed Stetzer, "The Epidemic of Bible Illiteracy in Our Churches," *Christianity Today*, July 6, 2015, christianitytoday.com/edstetzer/2015 /july/epidemic-of-bible-illiteracy-in-our-churches.html.

3. Dennis Prager, "The Missing Tile Syndrome," PragerU, August 4, 2014, https://prageru.com/videos/missing-tile-syndrome.

4. "How to Tame the Terrible Tongue," Keep Believing Ministries, May 10, 2017, keepbelieving.com/sermon/how-to-tame-the-terrible-tongue.

5. Adapted from L. B. Cowman, *Springs in the Valley* (Grand Rapids: Zondervan, 1939), 239.

Chapter 6 Walking in Freedom

1. Hara Estroff Marano, "Our Brain's Negative Bias," *Psychology Today*, last reviewed June 9, 2016, psychologytoday.com/articles/200306/our -brains-negative-bias.

Chapter 7 Self-Talk—We All Do It

1. Heather Holleman, *Seated with Christ: Living Freely in a Culture of Comparison* (Chicago: Moody, 2015), 69–70.

2. Linda Sapadin, PhD, "Talking to Yourself—A Sign of Sanity," Trans-4mind, accessed August 15, 2018, trans4mind.com/counterpoint/index -authors/sapadin13.shtml.

3. Wendy Komancheck, "Sonya Carson, Mother of Famous Neurosurgeon, Ben Carson," *History's Women*, accessed August 15, 2018, historys women.com/amazingmoms/SonyaCarson.html.

4. Evan Andrews, "7 Amazing Rags to Riches Stories," History, July 9, 2013, history.com/news/history-lists/7-amazing-rags-to-riches-stories.

5. "How Complaining Physically Rewires Your Brain to Be Anxious and Depressed," Daily Health Post, May 14, 2018, dailyhealthpost.com/complaining-brain-negativity.

6. Travis Bradberry, "How Complaining Rewires Your Brain for Negativity," Entrepreneur, September 9, 2016, entrepreneur.com/article/281734.

7. Sharyn Albright, On a Tightrope: Experiences with God (CreateSpace, 2016), 87–92.

Chapter 8 Fearfully and Wonderfully Made

1. Lana Heightly, Presents from on High: Freeing Women to Walk in Their Gifts (Lake Mary, FL: Charisma House, 2004).

2. Joseph Stein, Fiddler on the Roof (New York: Crown Publishers, 1964), 97–99.

3. Gary Chapman, The 5 Love Languages: The Secret to Love That Lasts (Chicago: Northfield Publishing, 1995).

Chapter 9 Freedom from Negative Self-Talk

1. Rick Warren, "It's Time to Eliminate Negative Self-Talk," Crosswalk, May 11, 2017, www.crosswalk.com/devotionals/daily-hope-with-rick-warren/daily-hope-with-rick-warren-may-11-2017.html.

2. LoriB, "James Pennebaker's Top Tips for Expressive Writing," Expressive Writing, June 30, 2014, expressivewriting.org.

3. Alice G. Walton, "6 Ways Social Media Affects Our Mental Health," Forbes, June 30, 2017, forbes.com/sites/alicegwalton/2017/06/30/a-run-down-of-social-medias-effects-on-our-mental-health/#6da5bbc32e5a.

4. Quoted in Carrie Kerpen, "Stop Comparing Your Behind-the-Scenes with Everyone's Highlight Reel," Forbes, July 29, 2017, forbes.com/sites/carriekerpen/2017/07/29/stop-comparing-your-behind-the-scenes-with-everyones-highlight-reel/#28a795e63a07.

Chapter 10 Life-Changing Words

1. Chen Miller, "Teacher in Israel Speaks about Education," Vimeo, accessed August 15, 2018, vimeo.com/195286745.

2. Rick Renner, "What Impression Do You Leave with Others?," R Renner, accessed August 15, 2018, renner.org/what-impression-do-you-leave-with-others, emphasis original.

3. Search Quotes, accessed August 15, 2018, searchquotes.com/quotation/Never_pass_up_an_opportunity_to_keep_your_mouth_shut./4267.

4. Reid Lamport, *Unleashing the Power of Encouragement* (Xulon Press, 2011), 141–42.

5. Lamport, *Unleashing the Power*, 142.

Chapter 11 Seeking the Forgiveness of Others

1. Charles Stanley, *The Gift of Forgiveness* (Nashville: Thomas Nelson, 1987, 1991), 7–8.

2. Matt Slick, "Is It Biblical to Forgive Ourselves?," Christian Apologetics and Research Ministry, accessed August 15, 2018, carm.org/questions/other-questions/it-biblical-forgive-ourselves.

3. Quoted in Josh Misner, "The One Thing Everyone Should Do after an Apology," *Time*, October 16, 2014, time.com/3513677/apologies-forg.

Chapter 12 Letting Go

1. "Maslow's Eight Basic Needs and the Eight Stage Developmental Model," The Mouse Trap, December 14, 2007, https://the-mouse-trap.com/2007/12/14/maslows-eight-basic-needs-and-the-eight-stage-developmental-model/.

2. Ekta R. Garg, "The #1inchlist," *The Writer*, October 16, 2017, https://www.writermag.com/2017/10/16/1inchlist/.

3. Brainy Quote, accessed August 15, 2018, brainyquote.com/quotes/napoleon_hill_152866.

Chapter 13 Free at Last

1. Quoted in Elisabeth Elliot, *Shadow of the Almighty: The Life & Testament of Jim Elliot* (New York: HarperOne, 1979), 212.

2. Desiree Ayres, *Beyond the Flame: A Journey from Burning Devastation to Healing Restoration* (Lake Mary, FL: Creation House, 2012), 72.

3. Ann Voskamp, *One Thousand Gifts: A Dare to Live Fully Right Where You Are* (Grand Rapids: Zondervan, 2010).

4. Christopher P. Neck and Charles C. Manz, *Mastering Self-Leadership: Empowering Yourself for Personal Excellence,* 6th ed. (London: Pearson Publishing, 2012), ix.

Final Words

1. Quoted in Cowman, *Springs in the Valley,* 368.

Mary C. Busha's first love is her husband, Bob, and her children and grandchildren. Her second love is her work, spanning over thirty-five years in the Christian publishing industry, where she has worn the hat of editor, agent, publisher, writers' coach, workshop presenter, and now full-time writer. Her work has appeared in periodicals such as *Writer's Digest* and *Focus on the Family*. Mary and Bob make their home in North Central Florida with their rescue dog, Missy, a miniature poodle, who has turned her owners' lives upside down in the most delightful ways. Mary can be reached by email at marycbusha@gmail.com.